The World Population Dilemma

POPULATION REFERENCE BUREAU, INC.

1755 Massachusetts Ave., N.W.
Washington, D. C. 20036

Columbia Books, Inc., Publishers
917 15th Street, N.W.
Washington, D. C. 20005

This book is part of a series. Other titles are:
People! (grades 7-9) and *This Crowded World* (grades 4-6).

Copyright © 1972

POPULATION REFERENCE
BUREAU, INC.

All rights reserved

Library of Congress
Catalog Number:
72-83500, SBN 910416-09-5

Price: $2.00 (paper)

Preface

"If Americans now and in future generations are to make rational decisions about their own and their descendants' future," says the 1972 final report of the Commission on Population Growth and the American Future, "they must be provided with far more knowledge about population change and its implications than they now possess." It goes on to say:

"There is no evidence that anything approaching an adequate population education program now exists in our schools. Very few teachers are trained in the subject and textual materials are scant and inadequate."

No area of human concern has a greater need for a rational, informed decision than that of population. Our finite planet cannot continue to accommodate increments to its population equivalent to a New York City every 40 days. Fragile landscapes cannot withstand the erosive impact of "boom and bust" communities, and the intensely focused pressures of rapid urbanization.

The processes of population growth, migration and settlement are propelled by individual choices. Technology in such areas as contraceptives, agricultural production and improved transportation can increase options, but ultimately there is the act of choice, and individuals must be prepared to choose intelligently. This means that individuals must come to recognize the future social consequences of personal actions, and be informed about what options are open to them.

The Population Reference Bureau for some years has believed what the Population Commission has enunciated—that primary and secondary schools are an indispensable vehicle for illuminating the facts and consequences of human population dynamics. These institutions are the most appropriate for equipping individuals to make choices among the range of available alternatives. In short, the schools of the United States play a central role in imparting to tomorrow's parents a sense of responsibility in light of the demographic circumstances.

Acting on this belief, in 1968, the Bureau's former president, Robert C. Cook, and Jane Lecht prepared an introduction to the study of population for students in grades 7 through 9, *People!*. In 1970, the Bureau published its second auxiliary text, *This Crowded World,* by Lillian B. Frankel, for students in grades 4 through 6. The present volume, the third in the series, has been prepared for both high school and college-level students. It is hoped that the factual explanation of human arithmetic, and a balanced discussion of the dilemmas to which it leads will create an awareness of the population dimension of human affairs. Such awareness will provide the student a basis for evaluating his own demographic circumstances and enable him to better respond with an intelligent choice.

This book is largely the work of Rufus E. Miles, past president of the Bureau, and some sections draw heavily on recent publications of the PRB which were authored by him. Additional material was contributed by the Bureau's managing editor, Carl E. Behrens. Much of the research for the book was developed by Roberta T. Williams, PRB research officer.

The Bureau is grateful to many education and population specialists for advice and suggestions in preparing this supplementary text. Special mention should be made of Dr. Noel-David Burleson of the Carolina Population Center, the University of North Carolina at Chapel Hill, and Dr. Edward L. Biller and Malcolm A. Dutterer of the Baltimore Public School System, who read and commented on an early version of the manuscript.

Michael F. Brewer
President

Contents

A note to the reader.

We frequently hear the phrase "population explosion" today. Newspapers use it . . . books are written about it . . . associations are formed to combat it. The number of humans occupying the planet, it is widely believed, has reached crisis proportions, and something—or many things—must be done to halt the human tidal wave.

Many individuals over the years have noted that population growth could not continue forever. In the last century particularly, there was much philosophical discussion about the forces that influence the growth of population. But it is only recently that population growth has become an urgent problem.

The urgency first came to the surface in underdeveloped countries, where efforts to improve the conditions of poor citizens were swamped by floods of the newly born. By the mid-1960s, this concern and urgency began to spread also to the industrialized countries. Even the United States, it was argued, was growing too fast for its own good.

Since the human race has survived for thousands of years, reproducing itself generation after generation, why has the problem of too many people only recently emerged as a threat to man's continued development? And what can he do about it?

A good place to start might be the Declaration on Population issued by UN Secretary General U Thant on Human Rights Day, December 10, 1966, and signed within a year by the heads of state of 30 countries.

"It took mankind all of recorded time until the middle of the last century to achieve a population of 1 billion. Yet it took less than a hundred years to add the second billion, and only 30 years to add the third. At today's rate of increase, there will be 4 billion people by 1975 and nearly 7 billion by the year 2000. This unprecedented increase presents us with a situation unique in human affairs and a problem that grows more urgent with each passing day.

"The numbers themselves are striking, but their implications are of far greater significance. Too rapid population growth seriously hampers efforts to raise living standards, to further education, to improve health and sanitation, to provide better housing and transportation, to forward cultural and recreational opportunities —and even, in some countries, to assure sufficient food. In short, the human aspiration, common to men everywhere, to live a better life, is being frustrated and jeopardized."

The statement asserts that "the opportunity to decide the number and spacing of children is a basic human right," and concludes with an appeal to leaders around the world to join in the development of family planning programs.

Since 1966, family planning has made a good deal of progress, although there is still more talk than there is action. But with progress has come controversy. More outspoken population experts argue that family planning is not enough—that people must be persuaded, and some extremists insist that they must be forced, to have fewer children. On the other side, there are those who dismiss the whole idea of a population crisis.

Whenever there is disagreement, there are problems of interpreting the facts. Especially in a number-clogged subject like population, it is easy to be confused when opponents in the controversy throw their challenges and counterchallenges back and forth.

This auxiliary text is aimed at making the reader familiar with a number of the ideas and concepts that are used in the discussion of population questions. And in doing so, it will bring into focus the facts of population growth that have led to what many people believe to be one of the most serious problems facing mankind: the World Population Dilemma.

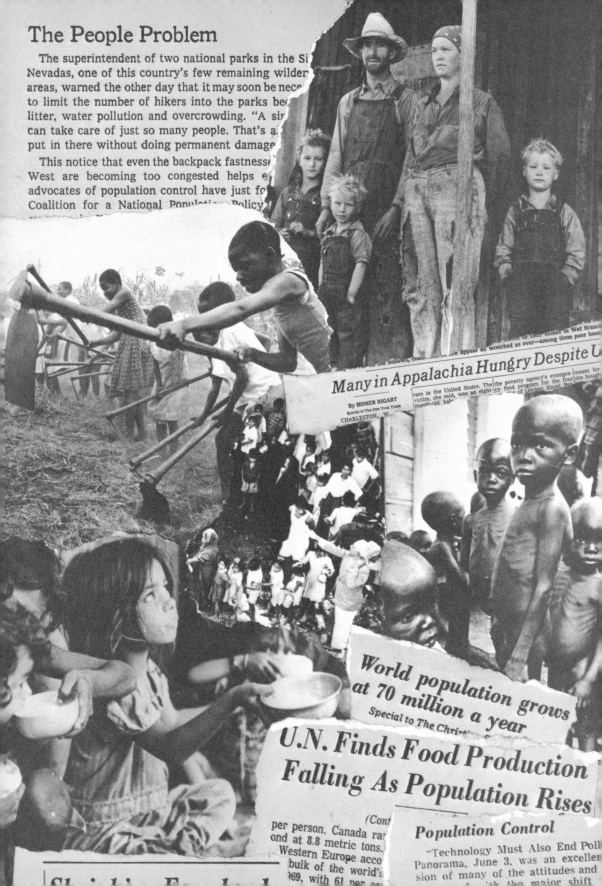

The People Problem

The superintendent of two national parks in the Si_____ Nevadas, one of this country's few remaining wilder___ areas, warned the other day that it may soon be nece____ to limit the number of hikers into the parks be____ litter, water pollution and overcrowding. "A si___ can take care of just so many people. That's a___ put in there without doing permanent damage____

This notice that even the backpack fastness____ West are becoming too congested helps e____ advocates of population control have just fo____ Coalition for a National Popul___ Policy___

Many in Appalachia Hungry Despite U___

By HOMER BIGART
Special to The New York Times
CHARLESTON, W___

rare in the United States. The victim, she said, was an eight-month-old bab___

the poverty agency's emergen-cy food program for the four___ of Letcher, Knott, Per___

meant for she bough___

World population grows at 70 million a year

Special to The Christ___

U.N. Finds Food Production Falling As Population Rises

(Cont___
per person. Canada ra___ ond at 8.8 metric tons.___ Western Europe acco___ bulk of the world's___ 969, with 61 per___

Population Control

"Technology Must Also End Poll___ Panorama, June 3, was an exceller___ sion of many of the attitudes and___ ___ the major shift

Chapter One

The Population Explosion – what it means

Looking at rapid worldwide population growth, it is possible to make a prediction: Sooner or later this growth will end—not for want of space, but for want of food, water and other natural resources, and possibly because of environmental pollution.

Population, when unchecked, increases in a geometric ratio. Subsistence increases only in an arithmetic ratio.—Thomas Malthus, 1798

When the English clergyman Thomas Malthus first brought the question of population growth into prominence more than a century and a half ago, he began a controversy that has lasted to the present day.

Malthus was writing at a time of great social change, when the French Revolution was changing men's ideas about social order and responsibility, and when England was beginning the great Industrial Revolution that was to change the economic and technological basis on which society was formed. The effect of population growth on these changes—and the effect of changing conditions on population growth —were topics discussed passionately throughout the 19th century and up to the present.

Population Growth Through the Ages

During the hundreds of thousands of years of the Old Stone Age when man was a hunter and a food gatherer, world population probably never exceeded 10 million. Then, sometime between 8000 B.C. and 6000 B.C., man learned to grow his own food, and to create settlements and eventually cities. In the next 8,000 to 10,000 years, his population increased fifty-fold, reaching an estimated 500 million by 1650 A.D.

This numerical advance could be called a population explosion in itself. But the term is generally applied to the even more rapid gain of the last three centuries.

In 200 years from 1650 to 1850, world population doubled and reached its first billion. In the next 80 years, it doubled again, and by 1975, given the present growth rates, it will have doubled once more to a total of 4 billion. By the year 2000 it will exceed 6 billion and possibly approach 7 billion unless there is a major reduction in birth rates or a major increase in death rates. If present trends continue, we will add, in a dozen years, 1 billion people—more than the total population of the earth little more than a century ago.

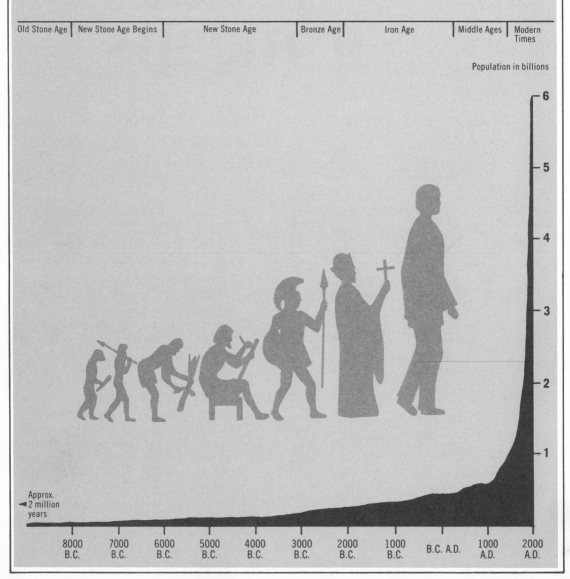

| Old Stone Age | New Stone Age Begins | New Stone Age | Bronze Age | Iron Age | Middle Ages | Modern Times |

Population in billions

6

5

4

3

2

1

Approx.
◄ 2 million
years

8000 B.C. 7000 B.C. 6000 B.C. 5000 B.C. 4000 B.C. 3000 B.C. 2000 B.C. 1000 B.C. B.C. A.D. 1000 A.D. 2000 A.D.

Malthus' main achievement was to point out that population growth must somehow be checked, or the numbers of people would soon outrun the supply of food. He estimated that without any checks on fertility, a population would double at a rate of about once every 25 years—which he called a geometric rate of growth. Agricultural productivity, on the other hand, would be hard put to keep up such a pace, he argued.

Malthus was much concerned with the checks that keep population from growing at a geometric rate. The arguments he made regarding checks to population growth were tied up with the issues of the day, and are not really relevant to a discussion of today's situation. But two points are important to note.

The first point is that world population today is growing at very close to Malthus' unchecked geometric rate. It will reach about 4 billion by 1975—more than four times what it was when Malthus wrote his first version of "An Essay on the Principle of Population" in 1798. And its present 2-percent growth rate, if continued, will cause it to double in 35 years—and quadruple in 70.

The second point to note is that food production has increased at a much more rapid pace than Malthus foresaw. Many millions of people are unfed and undernourished, and their numbers may well be increasing. But in the race between agricultural technology and population growth, food production has not yet been left hopelessly behind.

How long can the race between population and agriculture continue? The response to this question must come in a later chapter of the book. At this point we can only present some illustrations that indicate the dimensions of the population explosion, and where it is leading.

Two measures are helpful in predicting the future growth of a population: the birth rate—how fast people are being born—and the death rate—how fast they are dying. The difference between the birth rate and the death rate determines how fast population is growing—ignoring the effects of immigration and emigration.

Death rates can change unexpectedly when famine, disease or disaster strike suddenly. In underdeveloped countries, they have also changed rapidly since World War II, as public health measures reduced the mortality from many widespread diseases. In the industrialized countries, death rates change slowly, and more predictably. Birth rates are somewhat harder to predict. Even in the highly developed countries, they may increase rapidly for a time, and then with equal suddenness drop back down again. This is what happened during the U.S. "baby boom" which followed World War II. But the more we understand about birth rates and trends, the more likely we are to be able to make intelligent guesses as to what the future—at least the near future—will bring.

The United Nations has been a focus for collecting demographic data since its beginning in 1945, and UN statistics on a worldwide basis are probably the most reliable. Their data show that birth and death rates vary considerably over the world. The underdeveloped areas generally have very high birth rates and high death rates; the industrialized countries have somewhat lower birth rates and death rates.

Birth and Death Rates, by Area

In Africa, there are an average of 47 births per year for every 1,000 population in the area. Asia and Latin America have somewhat smaller birth rates, but they are still quite large—about 38 births per 1,000 population per year. In Europe and Northern America, on the other hand, the birth rate is considerably lower—about 18 per 1,000 population each year. These figures were based on data available in 1971.

Death rates also vary, being highest in Africa and Asia, and lower in other parts of the world.

The difference between birth rates and death rates is the rate at which population is growing —called the rate of natural increase. Worldwide, for each 1,000 persons, there are 20 more births than deaths a year—which means an increase of 2 percent a year in population.

2 births per 1,000 population   2 deaths per 1,000 population

AFRICA ← Growth Rate →

ASIA

LATIN AMERICA

WORLD AVERAGE ← World Growth Rate →

OCEANIA

EUROPE

NORTHERN AMERICA

U.S.S.R.

Projected Population Growth, 1970-1985

World population is expected to be almost 5 billion by 1985. Of this number, more than half will live in Asia. Africa and Latin America, with their high birth rates and declining death rates, are also expected to grow rapidly during this period. But even Northern America, with a growth rate of only 1 percent a year, is expected to have a population of about 280 million people by 1985.

Projected Population 1985

Population in 1970

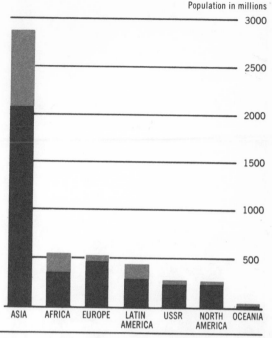

Population in millions

3000

2500

2000

1500

1000

500

ASIA   AFRICA   EUROPE   LATIN AMERICA   USSR   NORTH AMERICA   OCEANIA

Using information on births and deaths as well as various national censuses and other measures of population, the United Nations has computed estimates of population growth to 1985, for various regions. What shows up most dramatically is the tremendous population growth to be expected in Asia. Yet even in Northern America —where the growth rate is not as large as that of Asia, Africa and Latin America—a population of some 280 million people is expected by 1985.

Looking at this rapid worldwide growth, it is possible to make another prediction: Population growth sooner or later will end. Since the beginning of its existence, the human race has doubled its numbers 31 times. At its present rate, it is doubling every 35 years. If it were to double another 16 times, there would be only 1 square yard for every man, woman and child on earth.

This will never happen. Human population will stop growing long before 16 more doublings—not for want of space, but for want of food, water and other natural resources, and possibly because of environmental pollution.

How and when will the growth in man's numbers come to an end? And when it does come to an end, will world population level off and stabilize, or, having overshot the sustaining capacity of the earth, will it fall sharply back?

Before these questions can be answered, or even discussed, some explanation is needed of what has caused it to grow so rapidly up to now.

No simple explanation of the population explosion is possible. But among the major factors were the settling of the Western Hemisphere, and the industrial and technological revolution which swept the world—a process we will call the Great Transformation. Medical knowledge shared in this technological revolution. Techniques were developed that prevented or cured many diseases and increased lifespans throughout the world.

The impact of these changes on the world population is the subject of the following chapters.

Chapter Two

The Origins of the Population Explosion

Western civilization was transformed from a rural, agrarian society to an urban, industrial one. In the context of this industrial revolution, the present patterns of birth and death rates in the West were formed. And a population explosion in the rest of the world came from the sudden importation of Western technology into agrarian nations.

The Americas

Before Columbus opened the New World to European settlement, the population of the Western Hemisphere was low compared with all other major continents except Australia. It has been estimated that in the year 1600 the population of Northern America—north of what is now the Mexican border—was only about 1 million, and the population of Mexico and Central America, South America and the Caribbean Islands was not more than 12 to 14 million.

In the three and a half centuries following the European discovery of America, the population of Northern America grew from about 1 million to more than 225 million.

Where did all these people come from? Many, of course, were immigrants—mostly from England until the

15

early 1800s, then increasingly from Ireland and Germany, from Scandinavia, and later from the Mediterranean and Eastern Europe. America absorbed much of Europe's population growth during the time of the expanding frontier.

But natural increase—growth of numbers through reproduction—was also important. Large families were looked on as an economic asset by most American farm families during the 18th, 19th and early 20th centuries. Moreover, the people who came to settle in the United States tended to be young, and more likely to have children than those who remained in Europe. Data are sketchy and not too reliable for these early years, but they indicate that the birth rate was higher in America than it was in Europe. In 1840, for instance, there were about 50 babies born for every 1,000 people in the United States. In the North-West-Central European countries in the same year, the rate was about 30 per 1,000.

Latin America's population grew more slowly than Northern America's until the 20th century, when it passed the northern region's rate of gain and also surpassed it in absolute numbers. Today, Latin America has the most rapid growth rate in the world.

Over the last three and a half centuries, the population of the Western Hemisphere has increased to a number nearly equal to the total population of the earth in 1600.

What the world population would have been if the Americas had not been settled we can never know. It seems certain, however, that it is substantially greater because of the opening and exploitation of these two continents, primarily by Europeans. Although Asia today is numerically far more important (China and India each have larger populations than all of North and South America), the settlement of the Americas with people must be listed as one of the basic elements in the world population explosion.

Growth of the Americas

The population of what are now the United States and Canada grew from about 1 million in the year 1600 to more than 225 million today. During the period from 1790 to 1860 the population of the United States more than doubled every 25 years. The rate has since slowed down, but it is still high enough to double the population in 63 years. Latin America's population grew slower than Northern America's until the 20th century. In the year 1900, the population of Latin America was about 53 million. But today, Latin America has some 291 million people, and its growth rate, almost 3 percent each year, is the highest in the world.

In 1600, when the Americas began to be colonized, their population was approximately 15 million. By 1970 the area's population had increased to 660 million—44 times greater than in 1600.

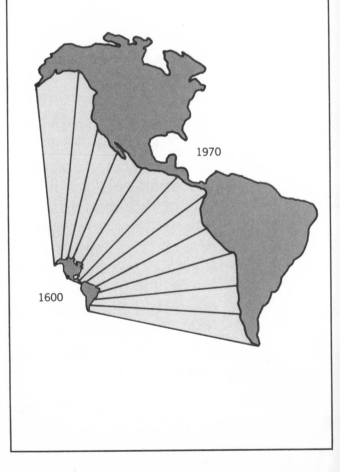

1970

1600

The Great Transformation

The filling up of the Americas was accompanied by a vast change in the social and economic patterns of the West during the 19th and early 20th centuries. Western civilization was transformed from a basically rural, agrarian society to a predominantly urban, industrial one. It was in the context of this Industrial Revolution that the present patterns of birth rates and death rates in the West were formed. And, as will be shown in the next section, the 20th-century population explosion in the rest of the world came largely as a result of the sudden importation of Western technology into agrarian nations without the corresponding introduction of the economic and social changes that took place during the West's Industrial Revolution.

There were four main features of the Great Transformation:

☐ **Agricultural productivity** was tremendously increased. This growth resulted from an expansion of cultivated land, from the use of fertilizer and finally from genetic improvements in crops and livestock.

☐ **Growing urbanization** accompanied the agricultural changes that made it possible to support more people with a smaller proportion of farm labor.

☐ **Fossil fuels**—coal and, later, oil —became the major source of power for manufacturing, transportation and many other purposes.

☐ **A managerial revolution** made it possible to sustain the network of personal, financial and organizational transactions that have been built up by the complexities of modern industrial civilization.

Not all of these factors, taken individually, had an easily seen effect on the growth of the world population in the last century and a half. But together they made the modern world and modern population growth possible.

Growth of Energy Use

The Industrial Revolution was built on the increased use of fossil fuels—first coal, then oil and gas. Power from hydroelectric projects, although sometimes locally important, contributes only a small share of world energy production. Nuclear power, still in its infancy, may become very important in future decades.

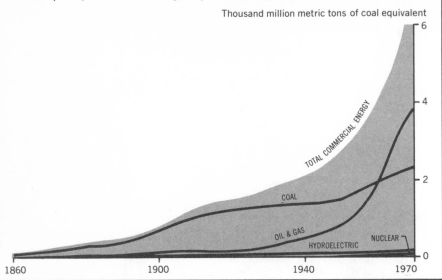

Thousand million metric tons of coal equivalent

Changes in agriculture, of course, did have a direct effect on population growth. Increased productivity per farm worker meant that more people who did not live on farms could be fed. (It also meant better nutrition and more resistance to disease, thus increasing the life span.) Many farmers migrated to the cities, where they provided labor for expanding industry.

The urban labor market was created by what might be called the power revolution. Before James Watt invented an economical steam engine in the late 1770s, the sources of power available to man were biologically renewable ones—human labor, domestic animals and combustible wood. Water-wheels and windmills and the sails of ships were also widely used, but they were secondary. The modern age, however, is the age of power from nonrenewable fossil fuels—primarily coal, gas and oil. Since Watt's invention, the increase in the use of power has been tremendous.

Fossil fuels, and the new machinery which they made possible, have led to one major industrial step after another. Each step has expanded—at least temporarily—mankind's capacity to feed, clothe, house and educate ever larger numbers of people.

Nonrenewable sources of power spurred the development of complex machinery and technology, which could supply the material needs of man with less human effort and in a shorter time than before. Steamships, for instance, could carry raw materials and finished products between the remotest part of the earth at speeds and in volumes scarcely dreamed of before. The 180-ton Mayflower took 66 days to cross the Atlantic in 1620; 20,000-ton freighters today can make the crossing in 5 days.

When electricity, the internal combustion engine, cars, trucks and airplanes came along, cities arose of a size that dwarfed ancient Rome—which had less than a million people in

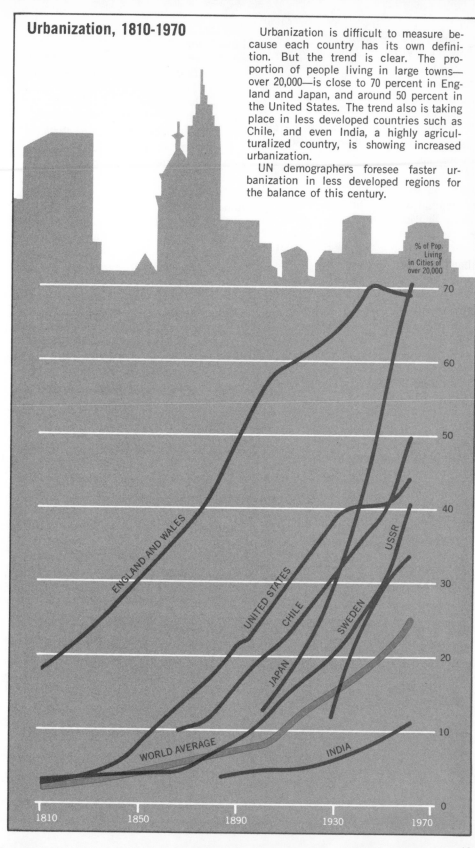

Urbanization, 1810-1970

Urbanization is difficult to measure because each country has its own definition. But the trend is clear. The proportion of people living in large towns—over 20,000—is close to 70 percent in England and Japan, and around 50 percent in the United States. The trend also is taking place in less developed countries such as Chile, and even India, a highly agriculturalized country, is showing increased urbanization.

UN demographers foresee faster urbanization in less developed regions for the balance of this century.

% of Pop. Living in Cities of over 20,000

70

60

50

40

30

20

10

0

ENGLAND AND WALES

UNITED STATES

CHILE

JAPAN

SWEDEN

USSR

WORLD AVERAGE

INDIA

1810   1850   1890   1930   1970

Imperial times. Super-cities, now often referred to as "megalopolises," became economically and technically supportable. Masses of humanity could live far from the source of their food and clothing and the materials with which their homes were built.

Urbanization and the Industrial Revolution could not have been sustained without the emergence of a high order of managerial and political skills. Managing all the transactions of a world population of more than 3.7 billion is a task that has been taken for granted, but is a fantastic feat. Without the very large jump in managerial expertise that has occurred in the last two centuries, the world would be more chaotic than it is. Its population, moreover, probably would not still be rising.

The Medical-Public Health Revolution

Industrialization, urbanization and the opening up of the Americas changed the basic patterns of civilization in much of the world during the 19th and early 20th centuries. These changes were accompanied by a great expansion of scientific knowledge and technology, including a revolution in the understanding, treatment and prevention of disease.

The fruits of this revolution have had a profound impact on population growth. As the new knowledge began to be applied, starting in the 19th century, death rates in Western Europe and the United States began to drop. During the mid-20th century, scientific advances were applied throughout the underdeveloped countries. Millions of lives were saved, and death rates fell even more abruptly. Because birth rates did not drop nearly as much,

Death Rates, 1770-1970 Developed Countries

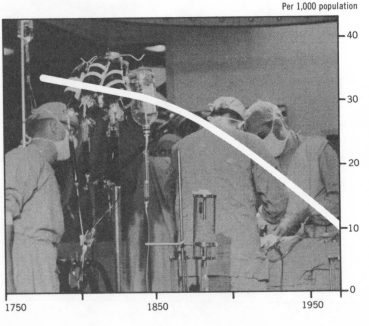

Per 1,000 population

Starting in the 1800s, death rates began to drop in the countries undergoing industrialization. This decline was quite slow. In several Western European countries, only about 85 percent of those born during the 1840s survived their first year of life, and about 65 percent lived to age 15. Death rates, however, continued to fall. A century later, 96 percent of all infants survived their first year, and about 75 percent lived at least to the age of 60. It is estimated that yearly deaths in the developed regions dropped from 28 per 1,000 population in 1850 to only 15 in 1950.

man's population has undergone an explosive growth.

The main achievements of the medical-public health revolution were vastly improved personal hygiene, cleaner food and drinking water, and the conquest of specific infectious diseases which had long plagued man. Although public hygiene had long been a concern, it was not until 1850 that the need to separate water supplies from sewage was firmly recognized. Before that time medical practice probably killed more people through insanitary conditions than it cured by treatment.

In the last half of the 19th century and well into the present one, the causes of a host of infectious killers—plague, yellow fever, cholera, typhus, amoebic and bacillic dysentery, tuberculosis and malaria—were identified and the means of controlling them were developed. For some diseases, notably malaria, effective control had to wait until after World War II.

Thus, in the developed world—primarily Europe and Northern America—famine was vastly reduced, and pestilence was largely controlled.* War and accidents remained as lessened but still significant causes of untimely death. With the near elimination of most serious infectious diseases, a high proportion of mortality in the industrialized world is caused by chronic and "stress" illnesses such as cancer and heart disease, which strike mostly at the older sectors of the population.

The situation has been much different in the underdeveloped world. There, until the end of World War II, only a slow decline in mortality took place; the decline was due in part to better control of epidemic diseases, including plague, smallpox and cholera.

---

* Influenza remains stubbornly recalcitrant, erupting every few years in a variant, immunity-resistant form that sweeps the world in pandemics reminiscent of the old days of plague and cholera. Although not a violent killer in itself, it causes many deaths from complications such as pneumonia.

Death Rates, 1770-1970
Underdeveloped Countries

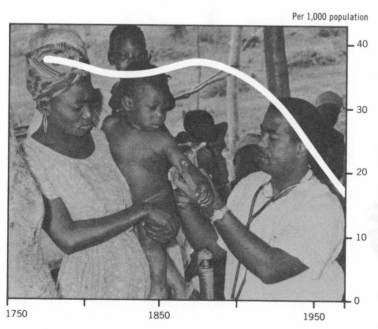

Per 1,000 population

The best calculations that demographers can make indicate that death rates in the underdeveloped world declined slowly but were still close to 30 per 1,000 in the 1940s. Following World War II, however, the decline in mortality became dramatically steeper. Ceylon's death rate, for example, fell from 19.8 to 14.0 in a single year, and in consequence the estimated expectation of life at birth soared from 43 years in 1946 to 52 years in 1947. In general, the annual death rate in the underdeveloped areas dropped from an estimated 28 per 1,000 people in the decade 1940-1950 to 17 per 1,000 in the decade 1960-1970.

1750   1850   1950

Infant Mortality, 1923-1968

Deaths among infants have a strong effect on population, since children who survive usually have children of their own. Infant mortality has been declining in underdeveloped areas since 1945. Among five less developed countries the average infant mortality rate went from about 150 per 1,000 live births in 1945 to 83 per 1,000 in 1968. Infant mortality for developed nations has declined more gradually, from about 35 per 1,000 live births in 1945 to about 20 per 1,000 in 1968.

Infant deaths per 1,000 live births

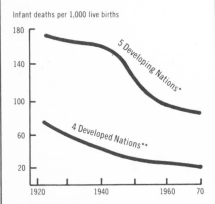

*Chile, Yugoslavia, U.A.R., Costa Rico, Mauritius.
**U.S.A., South Africa (European population), Sweden, New Zealand.

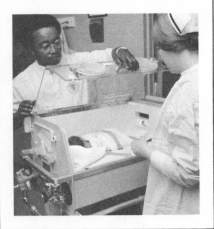

Following World War II, however, death rates fell rapidly. In many cases, this reduction in deaths resulted largely from the control of malaria, which was the world's single most potent cause of sickness and death before World War II. The widespread use of DDT, sprayed from airplanes, killed the mosquitoes that carry the disease and brought it under control in many areas. Other public health measures, such as improving water and food sanitation, were also introduced. Campaigns to control smallpox on a worldwide scale were undertaken; new antibiotics and sulfa drugs were used to control many infectious diseases.

As in the developed countries earlier, death rates among infants declined in the underdeveloped countries. A drop in infant mortality is especially important as a factor in population growth, since children who survive usually have children of their own. Although deaths among infants remain high in underdeveloped areas, the recent decline has been dramatic.

Birth and Death Rates, 1770-1970

In the industrialized nations in the last century, the declining death rate (see figures 7, 8, pages 20, 21) was accompanied by a decline in the birth rate. From a rate of about 40 per 1,000 in 1875, the birth rate in developed countries went down to about 20 per 1,000 by 1970. Demographers refer to this gradual shift in both birth and death rates as the "demographic transition."

The difference between the birth rate and the death rate is a measure of how fast the population is increasing. For developed countries, this difference is about 10 per 1,000 population, or about 1 percent. This means that despite going through the demographic transition, developed countries continue to grow in population.

In underdeveloped countries, the sharply dropping death rate has not been accompanied by a significant drop in the birth rate. In these countries, the birth rate has continued to be close to 40 per 1,000 while the death rate has fallen to about 15 per 1,000 in 1970. The result is an increase in population of about 25 per 1,000 population each year, or 2.5 percent.

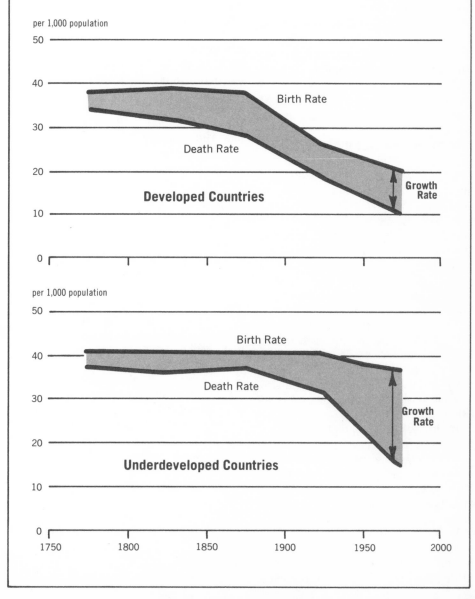

Fertility Trends—
The Demographic Transition

Death rates have fallen sharply all over the world—and the result has been what we call a population explosion. But birth rates are also important in determining population growth. What has happened to them while death rates were changing?

In the industrialized nations in the last century, and continuing in this one, declining mortality was accompanied by a gradual drop in the birth rate. Both of these declines were fairly slow, taking about a century and a half to reach their present levels. There was population growth, but it was moderate enough to be accommodated by expanding industrial economies—at least until recent years.

Demographers refer to this gradual shift of birth and death rates as the "demographic transition."

In the developing nations, the demographic transition of the West has not been duplicated. Mortality has dropped much more abruptly than it did in the industrialized world; more importantly, there has been no significant decline as yet in the birth rate, except in a few small countries such as Costa Rica and Taiwan, and possibly in Mainland China. The result has been a very rapid increase in population growth in the underdeveloped world.

There is much controversy about the demographic transition: what it means and what caused it. Most interesting is the question of whether the underdeveloped world, given time, could also spontaneously go through its own transition.

Basically, the demographic transition consists of decreasing mortality, with an accompanying rise in population, followed by a subsequent decline in fertility, particularly among the urban, moderately well-to-do, better educated sectors of the population.

In England, for example, the dynamism of the economy—the richest in the world at mid-19th century—made it possible for many lower-income people to join the middle class. Caring for large families at middle-class standards was an expensive proposition, however. One way of moving upward on the social scale was to limit the number of one's children.

These social factors, some demographers say, stimulated a decline in fertility even before the effects of falling mortality began to be felt. And when infant mortality began to decline, parents realized that more and more children were surviving. There was no longer any need to have six or seven children to guarantee the survival into adulthood of three or four. This factor, too, tended to reduce fertility.

As smaller families became prevalent among the middle-income groups, there occurred what has been termed the democratization of birth control—a movement to spread the word among all classes. The activities of Annie Besant and Charles Bradlaugh in the late 19th century in England and, a generation later, of Margaret Sanger in the United States, brought the advocacy of birth control into the open, where it has remained ever since, despite continued controversy.

The new trend was especially pronounced in the cities, which attracted ambitious people for whom small families became an advantage. This pattern was reinforced by the fact that unlike farm children, city children tended to be more of an economic liability than an asset. Housing shortages in cities may also have encouraged parents to limit their family size.

In general, annual births throughout the more developed regions dropped from about 34 per 1,000 population at the start of this century to 19 in 1970—a much faster decline than occurred in the preceding half century.

Desired Family Size, Selected Countries*

In countries with low birth rates, the number of children desired is considerably lower than in most underdeveloped countries. Among the countries in the first group, for instance, only Canada shows a desired family size of more than four children, and in most of these countries the desired number of children is less than three. Among the underdeveloped countries, the average desired family size is somewhere near four, and several countries have figures considerably greater than four.

*For various years, 1952-1964, depending on the country.

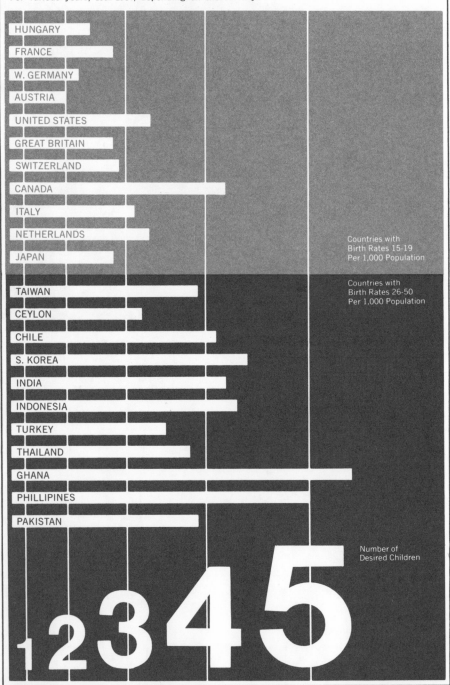

HUNGARY
FRANCE
W. GERMANY
AUSTRIA
UNITED STATES
GREAT BRITAIN
SWITZERLAND
CANADA
ITALY
NETHERLANDS
JAPAN

Countries with
Birth Rates 15-19
Per 1,000 Population

TAIWAN
CEYLON
CHILE
S. KOREA
INDIA
INDONESIA
TURKEY
THAILAND
GHANA
PHILLIPINES
PAKISTAN

Countries with
Birth Rates 26-50
Per 1,000 Population

Number of
Desired Children

1 2 3 4 5

Some of the factors that led to the demographic transition in industrialized countries are also becoming significant in the underdeveloped world. There is a sharp trend toward urbanization; industrialization is taking place more slowly. Infant mortality has dropped. In some countries, birth control information and materials are becoming available. As yet, however, these factors do not seem to have had much effect on cultural fertility patterns.

One of the best indications of the difference in cultural patterns is the number of children which adult men and women desire. In countries with low birth rates, this number is considerably lower than in most underdeveloped countries.

The increased population burden in the underdeveloped countries has led some of them to try to change cultural patterns. Billboards in India, for example, proclaim the message that two children are enough. In China, the radical social changes being introduced by the Communist regime appear to include encouragement of small families and delayed marriage. However, low literacy, limited funds and the lack of trained medical personnel often undermine these programs.

Governments have learned that it is much easier to achieve technical successes in mosquito eradication and mass vaccination campaigns than it is to change age-old behavioral patterns in the family. The result has been, and no doubt will continue to be for some years, an exploding population among those nations that can least afford it.

In this section it has been seen that the demographic transition of industrialized countries has not yet taken place in the underdeveloped world. Most observers would agree that the situation in these areas is too critical to depend on the possibility of a similar transition occurring as a consequence of widespread industrialization and urbanization. At current rates of development, that process is too slow. It is this feeling that is behind the urgent pleas and efforts now being taken to set up or greatly expand family planning programs in underdeveloped countries.

But what of the developed world? It is true that a transition toward lower birth rates took place, but they are still higher than the death rates. Population in these countries is still growing, and to those who are concerned about the population explosion, even the relatively moderate growth of countries which have gone through the demographic transition is too much.

Chapter Three

The Momentum of Population Growth

If each family decided to have no more than two children—enough to replace the parents—would population growth stop? No; not for many years.

The world is clearly in the grip of a population dilemma. The scale of the dilemma has been detailed in earlier chapters; the causes of it—the Great Transformation in society that brought about a decrease in death rates first in the West and then in the underdeveloped world—have been described. The fact that birth rates have also declined somewhat in industrialized countries was also brought out, as well as the important point that this demographic transition has not yet taken place in the rest of the world.

There seems to be wide agreement that population growth should be slowed. But what if everyone accepted the need to limit childbearing, and was willing to translate that need into his own personal terms? If each family decided to have no more than two children—enough to replace the parents—would population growth stop?

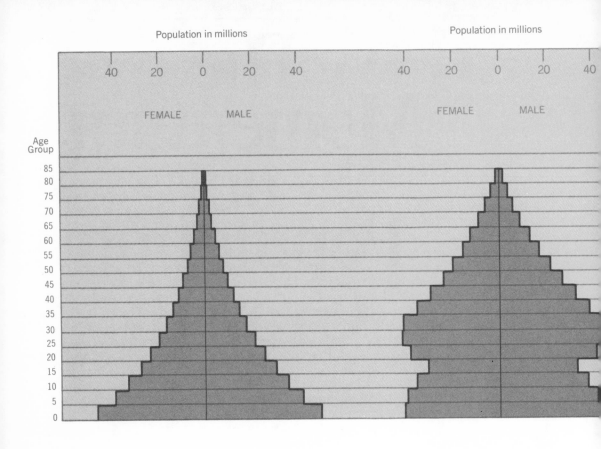

Population in millions

Population in millions

| 40 | 20 | 0 | 20 | 40 | | 40 | 20 | 0 | 20 | 40 |

FEMALE   MALE

FEMALE   MALE

Age Group

85
80
75
70
65
60
55
50
45
40
35
30
25
20
15
10
5
0

INDIA: AGE DISTRIBUTION
1970

PROJECTION
YEAR 2000

If Birth Rate drops to replacement level by 1985

India: Growth and Age Structure, 1970-2000

A good way to see the effect of age structure is by using an age pyramid, in which the number of people in each 5-year age group is represented by a horizontal bar. In India, and in other countries where population growth has been rapid, the number of people in the low age groups is much greater than the number in the higher age groups. In 1970, there were almost 100 million children under 5 years old in India, less than 50 million in the 20-25 age group, and something less than 25 million in the 40-45 age cohort. Each year, the number of young people who become parents is much greater than the number of parents who move out of their reproductive years. If present birth and death rates continue,

Population in millions

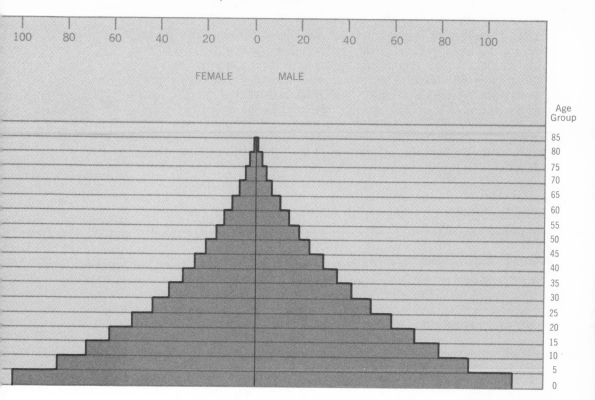

| 100 | 80 | 60 | 40 | 20 | 0 | 20 | 40 | 60 | 80 | 100 |

FEMALE   MALE

Age
Group

85
80
75
70
65
60
55
50
45
40
35
30
25
20
15
10
5
0

PROJECTION
YEAR 2000

If present Birth
and Death Rates
continue

in the year 2000 there will be nearly 215 million children under 5 years old, more than 110 million people in the high reproductive years of 20-25, and something like 50 million in the 40-45 age group whose childbearing years are just about over. At these rates, India's population will reach 1.2 billion by the end of the century.

Even if Indian parents should decide by 1985 to have mostly two-child families—an optimistic as-

sumption—the momentum of the present population boom would be felt for decades. Under these conditions the population would increase from its present 570 million to 890 million by the year 2000, and would continue to increase until about the year 2035, by which time the population would be 1.2 billion. During all that time, Indian families would have to limit their size to close to two children each; otherwise, the population would rise even higher.

The answer to that question is: No, not for many years.

Population would continue to grow for decades because of the momentum built up by the rapid growth of the present generation. The momentum comes from the large number of young people who are present in a rapidly growing population. It is an illustration of *how age structure affects population growth*.

The age structure of a population is usually represented in a diagram called an "age pyramid," in which the number of people in each 5-year age group—called a cohort—is represented by a horizontal bar. In underdeveloped countries with high fertility, there are a great many young children relative to the total population. In rapidly growing countries, young people under 15 years of age account for 40 − 45 percent of the total population.

As these children grow up, they move into their reproductive years. At the same time, the age group or cohort that has been having babies grows too old to have more. But because the younger cohort is more numerous than the older one, there will be more of them to have babies. Even if they are less fertile than their parents, they probably will produce more babies altogether.

India is an example of the continuing effect of age structure on population growth. Even if Indian parents were to decide by 1985 to have mostly two-child families, the country's population would continue to grow until the year 2035. By that time, unless death rates increased, there would be about 1.2 billion Indians. That is more than twice the present population of that overcrowded country.

The momentum of population growth can also be seen in the aftereffects of the post-World War II baby boom of the United States. Here the rapid growth was caused not by a sharp drop in mortality, as in the case of the underdeveloped world, but by a sharp increase in fertility.

Here again, as in India, population growth would continue even if U.S. parents had no more than enough children to replace themselves. Because of the great bulge of the population now entering the reproductive age—those who were born during the baby boom—growth would not be halted unless families had an average of 1.2 children each. Such a pronounced reduction in fertility could occur, of course, but it is unlikely.

Age Structure in the United States

Population momentum is also evident in the U.S. age pyramid. During the years from 1946-1965, the so-called "baby boom" resulted from very high birth rates. The birth rates began to fall in the mid-1960s, so that the age pyramid shows a bulge for baby-boom years.

But even if the average number of children women bear continues at its present lower level, the bulge of the baby-boom years will be reflected in greater numbers of children in the last part of the century.

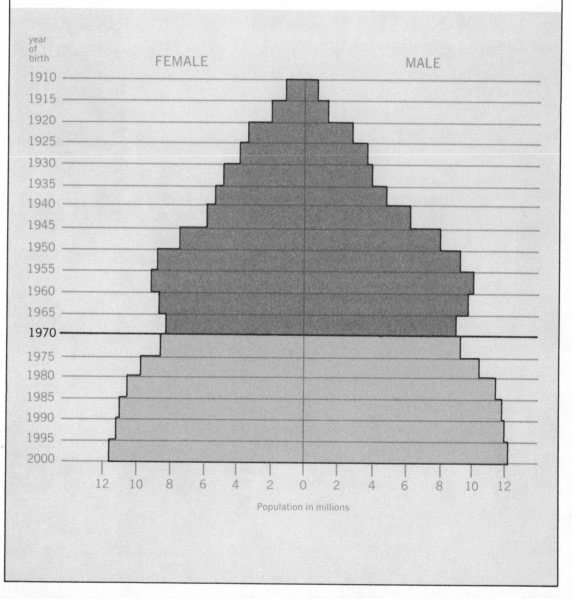

Population in millions

Chapter Four

Population in Perspective

People who have been brought up in the industrialized West usually expect science to solve the most complex problems. But technological solutions are stopgap solutions; as population increases, the solutions become less sufficient, and new ones must be found.

Is Science the Answer?

Why are many population specialists concerned about the rapid growth of the past few decades?

Their ultimate concern, of course, is the threat of widespread starvation. With many millions of people undernourished at the present time, they consider rapid population growth a serious threat to the ability of the world's agriculture to produce at even the present individual consumption levels, much less improve nutrition.

The tremendous momentum of population growth, described in the last chapter, increases the worry about food supplies. Economic, biological or physical events could cause agricultural production to drop; and this could happen at such short notice that the momentum of population growth could not adjust to it. Widespread famine could be the result.

There are other concerns, besides the threat that population will outrun food supplies. Rapid population growth in the less developed countries is undermining efforts to bring these areas out of the well of poverty which they now occupy—efforts that will have great significance for the future peace and stability of the world's societies. And in the industrialized countries, population growth is aggravating one of the world's most serious problems: the growing burden of pollution on the earth's natural ecosystem. Closely related to the environmental problem is the question of mass production and mass consumption—principles on which the prosperity of the industrialized world so far has depended.

The aim of this chapter is to examine each of these major world problems and discuss how population growth affects the outcome of efforts to solve them.

Agriculture

Although a great deal more food would be needed to provide adequate nourishment—in quantity and in quality—for the people of the rapidly growing nations of the world, agricultural production has kept pace with even the accelerated population growth of the last several decades. This does not mean that starvation has disappeared, for the increased production of food has not always occurred where the demand was located, and its distribution has been often slow and inefficient. Nevertheless, agricultural output has increased in recent years. Crop yields in the United States and other parts of the world have increased dramatically. Production of poultry and livestock has become highly systematized. New strains of wheat and rice give promise of a short-term gain in nutrition in some areas where it is needed most—in the Far East and in Latin America.

There is no way of predicting how long agricultural production can keep pace with population growth. Efforts to increase agricultural production consist of two parts: short-run improvements in the efficiency and distribution of conventional crops and foods, and long-run projects to develop new sources of food.

In the short run, subtropical agriculture is on the brink of a substantial increase in production of staples so promising that it has been called the "Green Revolution." New strains of wheat, rice and corn, particularly applicable to tropical climates, are expected to increase yields where they are effectively utilized.

The new strains involved in the Green Revolution often require a more precise timing of planting and irrigation, as well as the application of large amounts of fertilizer, and other changes from traditional agricultural practices. In fact, getting tradition-bound farmers to adopt the new technologies needed by Green Revolution agriculture may be as difficult as changing tradition-bound family patterns that

Population and Food Production

During the rapid increase in population of the last two decades, the world's agriculture has also increased production. And the development of new strains of wheat and rice for tropical climates promises to increase yields where they are most needed.

But clearly the gains from this new technology —called the Green Revolution—will not last forever. Dr. Norman Borlaug, who played an important role in developing the new strains, says that they have given the underdeveloped countries a breathing space of perhaps 30 years to bring their population growth down.

Index
(1952-'56 = 100)

140

120

FOOD PRODUCTION

POPULATION

PER CAPITA FOOD PRODUCTION

100

80

1948-'52
Average

1955

1960

1965

1970

Grain Yield Per Acre

Modern farming methods, including improved seeds and pesticides and heavy applications of fertilizer, have boosted the amount of grain obtained from an acre of land in many advanced nations. The Green Revolution promises to bring similar improvements—not reflected in the graphs—to a number of subtropical areas.

So for a few decades, the race between population and agricultural technology may continue to be neck and neck. But many people are questioning whether the population-technology race, like the international arms race, is not consuming an unreasonable share of man's efforts and resources.

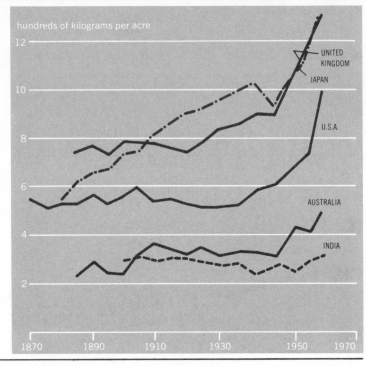

contribute so much to high fertility in many developing countries. Still, the new strains of wheat and rice have sharply increased grain production in several less developed countries, and have provided a cushion against starvation which had not previously existed.

Nobel Prize winner Norman Borlaug, who had much to do with developing the new strains of cereals behind the Green Revolution, estimates that, if adopted, the new agriculture may give mankind a 30-year breathing spell during which widespread famine can be staved off. After that time, unless population growth is curtailed, another agricultural crisis would be upon us. To meet it—to avoid famine—new sources of food would have to be found. What might they be?

Ideas for new food sources range from the ambitious to the bizarre. Many of them revolve around the sea: fish farming; the development of a high-protein flour called Fish Protein Concentrate (FPC); the conversion of plankton, microscopic organisms of the ocean, into palatable food. Scientists

are even talking about converting coal into body-building nutrients. Another proposal is to grow large fungus-type plants, like mushrooms, on a petroleum base.

All of these hopes deserve careful examination. Some of them probably will prove to be practical and economical; some presently unthought-of source of sustenance for mankind may be developed.

Another direction that agriculture might take in the pursuit of food for the coming billions of men could be the reclamation of desert areas. Some work along this line has been undertaken in Israel and in other arid places.

The most ambitious proposal in this direction has been what scientists at the Atomic Energy Commission call an "agro-industrial complex." This concept is built around huge nuclear power plants that would be used to desalt ocean water for irrigation and produce electric power for industrial purposes. Coastal areas, particularly in the tropics, might be converted from desert to fertile agricultural regions through the availability of ample nuclear power, according to this idea.

So far plans to go ahead with this kind of project on an operational basis have been stalled by high costs, the possibility of environmental damage and safety problems. On the other hand, researchers are going ahead with experiments in agriculture under conditions in which they have complete control of the amount of water and nutrients available to the crops they are growing. This kind of complete control presumably would be possible within an agro-industrial complex, and the expected high yields from such a no-lack agriculture would be one of the major advantages of the system.

Beyond these highly theoretical proposals for adding to the world's food supply, it is impossible to see. Technology has changed so quickly in the past that predictions of the far future are not very fruitful. It is conceivable that future crises in world food supplies might be temporarily staved off, just as the Green Revolution seems to be staving off the present one.

But these increases in food supply obviously cannot keep occurring indefinitely. There is bound to be an upper limit, and when that limit is reached, or perhaps sooner, world population growth must end.

Many people believe today that we are close to that upper limit. Others, counting on further technology, disagree. But a growing number of observers are beginning to view the situation not in technological terms, but from a social and economic aspect. Regardless of the possibilities of unknown future agricultural breakthroughs, they question the logic of the desperate race by technology to catch up with the ever increasing burden of population growth. If population growth were reduced, they argue, the efforts and resources now absorbed by the race could be better directed toward solving some of the other problems of world society. This is a point that we will return to later in this chapter.

Population and World Poverty

Food is not the only concern of the underdeveloped world, although it is a paramount one. These nations, many of them created from former colonies, have been attempting to improve their economic situation by changing their basic role in the world economy. Before World War II, many underdeveloped areas were sources of raw materials for the developed world—metal ores, oil and basic food products. They imported manufactured goods at relatively high cost. Large sectors of their populations, living in rural areas, subsisting on their own agricultural production and acquiring other commodities through barter or trade, had practically no money income. The major thrust of economic development in recent decades has been toward industrialization and bringing larger numbers of people into a money economy.

These efforts have brought about some improvement. The economies of the poorer nations, as measured by "per capita income"—the average income of individual citizens—have expanded, and industrialization has gained a tentative foothold. But per capita income in these countries has not increased nearly as rapidly as in developed countries. The global income gap has widened, not narrowed.

Population growth obviously has a direct effect on per capita income, since greater numbers mean that the total national income must be divided into smaller pieces.

But population growth influences national economic development in more ways than just the simple measure of per capita income. Increasing numbers of people impose increased burdens on the economy. In rural areas, rapidly increasing population puts pressure on local agriculture to support more people, decreasing the amount of output that enters the national market. Population pressure, coupled with the urge to obtain some of the advantages such as education and

Income and Population Growth Compared

Since 1945, underdeveloped countries have made considerable efforts to industrialize and increase their income. These efforts have been somewhat successful—the total gross product of underdeveloped countries has increased from something like $150 billion in 1950 to a little more than 500 billion in 1968. Meanwhile, however, the developed countries have increased their income from a little more than $700 billion in 1950 to more than $1,500 billion in 1968.

More dramatically, population in underdeveloped countries more than doubled from a figure of 1.2 billion in 1950 to 2.5 billion in 1968. In the developed countries, population increased from 500 million in 1950 to about 750 million in 1968.

One way of measuring a country's prosperity is by per capita income—the amount of income divided by the population. In these terms, underdeveloped countries increased their per capita income from $125 per person per year to $200. At the same time, however, the developed countries increased their per capita income from $1,400 to $2,000. Thus the underdevelopment gap, as measured by per capita income, has increased rather than decreased.

Developed Countries	**Underdeveloped Countries**
1950	
1968	

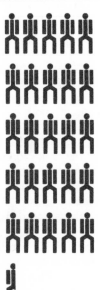

 100 million population

$100 billion total GNP

improved health care that are available only in the cities, has contributed to a high rate of urbanization in developing countries. Mass migration to the cities places a heavy burden on available social services, and also results in heavy unemployment or underemployment.

It is here that population growth is particularly serious. Because of the built-in momentum of population growth, the labor force will continue to expand rapidly, adding to an unemployment problem that is already critical in most underdeveloped countries.

Population and Environment

Problems of food and unemployment are less serious in the industrialized countries. In fact, in the United States a highly efficient agriculture is actually subsidized to keep production down and prices up. The substantial poverty and malnutrition that unfortunately still exist in the United States are not due to low production but to a faulty system of distributing food and purchasing power to low-income people. To many Americans, personally more concerned with overeating than with lack of food, the question of sustenance seems rather remote.

But other problems are becoming more serious. One that is gaining increasing attention today is the threat to the environment posed by the increasing affluence of increasing millions of citizens in industrialized countries.

People cause pollution, and it might be expected that more people would mean more pollution.

To some degree this is true, but the formula is not that simple. The amount of pollution depends not only on how many people there are, but what they are doing, and how they are doing it.

In the case of agriculture, for instance, it has been seen that the production of foodstuffs has been greatly increased over the last several decades —and promises to increase still further —through the application of modern agricultural techniques. But these same techniques contribute heavily to pollution in a number of ways. They require heavy inputs of fertilizer, more than the crops and the soil can absorb. Fertilizers often are washed off the land into waterways, where they cause the rapid growth of algae—small water plants— contributing to the clogging up and eventual death of many lakes and ponds. Modern agriculture also depends on widespread use of pesticides, some of which—including DDT—are severe pollution threats on a global scale. There is also a pollution component to the reclamation of nonfertile lands—the agro-industrial complex already mentioned. Desalting water for irrigation takes great amounts of power, as does the production of fertilizer.

Power production, in general, is one of the most serious contributors to pollution, particularly air pollution. Most power today is produced by burning fossil fuels, coal or oil. Fossil fuel plants contribute heavily to air pollution. Nuclear power doesn't contribute as much to air pollution, but it has two other major drawbacks: It produces large amounts of radioactive wastes, some of which remain active, or lethal, for hundreds of years; and it produces much excess heat which must be dissipated. The widespread construction of nuclear reactors poses serious problems of heat pollution which could affect waterways, wildlife and even climate. And no one has yet figured out what is to be done with radioactive wastes.

Industry, of course, is also a major contributor to pollution. Not only do the industrial processes contribute heavily to water and air pollution, but the products that they manufacture—particularly automobiles but also products such as throwaway bottles and laundry detergents—pollute the air and water and contribute to growing mountains of solid waste that are increasingly difficult to bury.

Population and Economics

Modern industry, particularly in the United States, is based on the idea of mass consumption. The efficiency and ideology behind competitive markets and mass production industry imply that it is better to produce many items at a price that large numbers of people can afford than it is to produce only a few items and sell them at such prohibitively high prices that only the wealthy can buy them.

This system has been enormously successful, bringing prosperity to unprecedented numbers of people. But it has also contributed to a psychological bent that idealizes growth as the cornerstone of the economy. Unless sales are continually expanding, unless production increases, the economy is in poor shape, according to this kind of reasoning.

The trouble with the concept of a growing economy is that the processes of production and consumption yield trash, wastes and other residuals as well as the goods and services we find valuable. As has been seen, electric power production generates both heat and air pollution; automobile emissions are one of the major contributors to air pollution; even soft-drink bottles cause pollution. Many ecologists believe that environmental pollution can be brought down to a safe level only if consumption is reduced, rather than increased.

Increasing per capita consumption is a major factor in a growing economy, but increasing population is also clearly related to it. In fact, population growth is a strong stimulus to expansion-minded industry. The prospect of ever increasing numbers of customers leads power companies to project ever increasing demands for electricity; it stimulates auto manufacturers to forecast markets for cars beyond the glut that now exists. Almost all major industries look on population growth as the cornerstone of future economic growth.

Reducing consumption in itself will not control pollution problems. Many

Air Pollution in Los Angeles

Because of its climate and geography, Los Angeles was one of the first areas of the nation to develop the kind of air pollution typical of an automobile society. Two main components of air pollution are hydrocarbons and nitrogen oxides. Despite efforts to control emission of these pollutants, the total load in Los Angeles County air continued to rise through 1970.

More stringent controls on automobile emissions, combined with a slowing of the rapid migration to California of the previous decades, will probably lead to a decrease in hydrocarbon and nitrogen oxide emissions by 1980. But after that, they can be expected to increase again.

The projections to 1980 and 1990 assume that the population predictions of the California State Department of Finance will be realized; that production of emissions will continue to increase relative to population as they have since 1950; that motor vehicle crankcase emissions will be 80 percent controlled, exhaust and evaporation hydrocarbons 70 percent controlled, and exhaust nitrogen oxides 60 percent controlled by 1980; and that no other controls will be adopted.

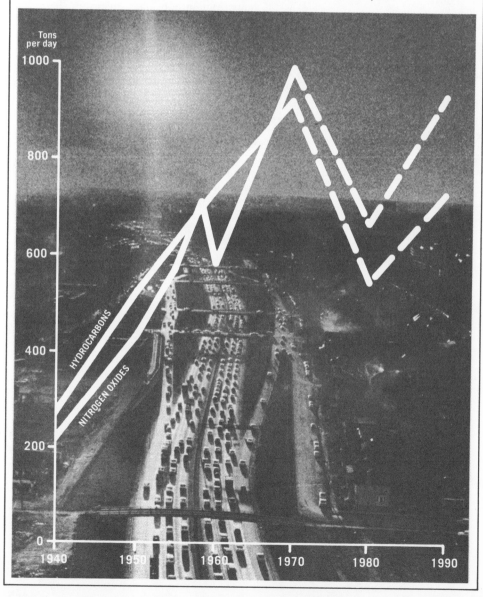

changes in production methods, in management of wastes and in recycling technology are needed to halt environmental deterioration. But reducing population growth, in this context, can be considered part of a general plan for reducing pollution and helping to cut down the overall consumption of energy and material goods which is at the root of pollution.

Nevertheless, the transition to a low-consumption economy will be difficult. The idea that static or declining population and consumption might be good for the economy will be hard to accept for industrialists who have built their careers on ever expanding sales. A lively debate is beginning, and no doubt will continue, about the effects of a declining population on economic prosperity. The decline of the growth-is-good psychology is likely to be one of the most profound changes in modern industrial society in the next few decades.

Technology and Population

Throughout the discussion of population and its related problems we have referred to various technological advances that promise to ease some of the negative effects of population growth. People who have been brought up in the industrialized West usually expect science to solve the most complex problems, and scientists have, in fact, achieved miraculous gains in many fields.

It is becoming obvious, however, that technological solutions to problems frequently bring problems of their own—particularly environmental problems. What is more, technological solutions are stopgap solutions. A world food crisis looms: Technology rushes in with a solution that staves it off for a few years. Industrial pollution threatens: Technology is called in to suppress or dispose of the pollutants, or to reduce the amount of pollution that is generated. As population and consumption increase, however, the stopgap solutions become ineffective, and the race is on once more.

Earlier in this chapter we referred to the race between population and food technology. This idea can now be broadened: It is a race between technology on the one hand and increasing population and consumption on the other. Some people are beginning to draw a parallel between this race and the nuclear arms race, and are questioning the logic of pursuing both of them. By producing more numerous and powerful armaments the great powers maintain their relative position and preserve an uneasy security. By attacking world problems of increasing population and consumption through technology, the world temporarily maintains its uneasy position on the edge of catastrophe. In the process both races undoubtedly provide many people with a livelihood, and some people with prosperity.

But the population-consumption-technology race, like the arms race, contains great dangers for mankind. What is more, both must end eventually. Could not the vast and desperate efforts of so many people who are involved in them be redirected to more fruitful, more satisfying directions?

W BIRTH CURB NDERGOING TEST

Lack of Side Effects in the Method Is Claimed

y SANDRA BLAKESLEE
Special to The New York Times

ALO ALTO, Calif., Sept. 25
new birth control method,
ose develope
e no side e
ed on 1,000
ted States a
he techniqu
the Alza
o Alto, which
develop way
delivery of
an system.
a idea is to
an directly
rest of the
sible.
he company'
ceptive Syst
principle. T
flexible,
ed drug pac
d directly i

three-day
by the Wome
on Coalition, drew a reg-
on of 1,025 women from
ates to MacMillan Audi-
n of Columbia University.
ended in some disorder
representatives claiming
peak for nearly a fourth of
e attending took over the
rophones to announce their
ndrawal after a d
s guarante
ual

How many children should a couple have?

Three? Two? One? None? There's no right answer.
It depends on how many children they really want.
How many children they feel they're ready for—
emotionally, and

them.
for the effect
on of how many

Parenthood
oice. Not chance.

---

7 wrong reasons for having a baby:

1. "You're married a year now. When are you young to give us grandchildren."

2. "You want to have a kid, Evelyn? All right, we'll have a kid. Maybe that'll patch things up."

3. "Why knock myself out working when I can have a baby?"

4. "I bet my parents would send us money if we had a baby..."

5. "Heh-heh, hey Frankie, what are you and Marcie waiting for?"

6. "We only want two kids. But if we don't have a boy we'll keep trying."

7. "Sure I want babies. What else is a woman for?"

These are just seven of the many wrong reasons for having a baby.
There's only one right reason: because you really want one.
And the right time is when you want one. When the baby can be a welcome addition, not an accidental burden.
Unfortunately lots of people who think they know how to

Planned Parenthood is a national, non-profit organization dedicated to providing information and effective means of family planning to all who want and need it.

An unexpected child can really rock the cradle.

That's because, no matter what a family's income is, it costs a lot of money to raise a child to age 18.
Many thousands of dollars more than most people think.
Which is why we advise every couple to plan when they want children: when they can be a welcome addition. Not an accidental burden.

Planned Parenthood
Children by choice. Not chance.

Old family-life concept crumble in modern Jap

By Reuter

Tokyo

The age-old oriental concept of family life is crumbling in the face of modern Japan's economic progress, according to a recent government report.

A white paper prepared by Japan's Economic Planning Agency (EPA) said democratic reforms in the post-World War II era emphasized the indivi rather than the

the rebelliousness and pe postwar young.
The breakup of the old is shown in National (NPA) figures for young ning away from home

More runaways

In 1966 the NPA recorded aways. Last year
dron

FDA Proposal on IU

By Morton Mintz

For the first time, the government is proposing to require makers of some intrauterine devices (IUDs) to demonstrate safety and efficacy before putting the birth-control devices on sale.
The proposal applies, however, only to experimental IUDs containing copper or other metal, or impregnated with a hormone or drug. At

Alza Corp., a California firm.
Searle, in March, announced plans to sell, through physicians, an IUD consisting of a piece of flexible plastic in the shape of a "7" with copper covering most of the 1½-inch-long stem.
The company had planned to introduce the

copper absorbed
sainly
won
devi
the
iver
earle
sainly
won
devi
the
iver

copper absorbed
can cause nerve
other adverse e
says that coppe
present in the
uterus, and that
released by the
the body each
50 one-millionth
—compared with
food, plus 40
water.

they had been
improper IUI
"closed" desig
le devices, or
insertion instr

What a pity that having children is often more important than wanting them.

The pressures for having children are great.
Some are social. Like a mother-in-law asking she's going to see grandchildren.
Or an aunt wondering but loud whether the couple is selfish.
Other pressures are personal. Like the self-doubt in many men and women over whether they actually can "make" a baby.
Other pressures are less obvious.
Like legal restrictions on the availability of birth control information, sex education in schools, and abortion. Not enough family planning services and needs thwarted.
As we said, the pressures are great.
But as far as we're concerned,

There's only one, repeat one, reason for a couple to have a child: because they really want it.
And are ready for it: emotionally, not just financially.
And there's only one time to have that child: when they want it. When it can be a welcome addition rather than an accidental burden.

Unfortunately, research has consistently shown that not enough American from every walk of life are aware of the benefits of family planning or how to go about it.
That's what we're all about. And frankly, we can use all the help we can get.
Especially from thoughtful people who understand how unplanned pregnancies can literally the already severe problems our society has still to solve.
People who will, at the very least, help others understand that there's a difference between having children—and wanting them.

Planned Parenthood
Children by choice. Not chance.

For a free booklet, "Scientist Ways You Can Help" write Planned Parenthood, Box 500, Radio City Station, New York, New York 10019.

Get to know the two of you before you become the three of you.

Get to know what you both really like.
What you both really want out of life.
Get to enjoy your freedom together until you both cide you want to let go of it.
ut make it your choice.
esearch statistics show that more than half of all regnancies each year are accidental. Too many m, to couples who thought they knew all about planning methods.
know how the ou don't have to e three of you. ur of you. Or...

Planned Parenthood
Children by choice. Not chance.

SINGLE IS CALMER

Men and wo
who remain
single are
less psych
logically distressed tha
those who marry, accordi
to a recent U.S. Public
Health Service survey.

The study shows that at
all ages, single persons
have less nervousness, les
fear of nervous breakdown.
less dizziness. fewer head
aches and f

More Men Having Birth Control Surgery

several area hospitals where report an increase in

fact that we've had many, many more requests for vasectomies in the past year," said Marjorie executive director

ciate professor of urology. Before 1970, he said, the hospital did perhaps one a month, usually to prevent disease or infection rather than as a birth-control Dr. Fresilli charges

medical need is indicated, not as a population control method.
At D.C. General Hospital, vasectomies solely for the purpose of population control are generally forbidden, according to the chief accident in urology. The head of

said he plans to review its po on sterilization.
The Office of Economic Opportunity, the federal anti-poverty agency, changed its policy in May to permit use of family planning funds for voluntary sterilization of men and women in low-income families. Dr. Contis, director of the

ecto.
opened
week had s
list, accord
the

Chapter Five

Population in the United States

The key question is whether the population problem would be solved if all methods of birth limitation were universally available. The answer to this question hinges on how many children parents WANT to have.

Although nearly everyone agrees that countries such as India and Pakistan have a grave population problem, concern about population growth in industrialized countries, particularly the United States, is much less common and much more recent. Little public discussion was given to the question until 1965 and 1966, when it became the subject of lengthy Senate hearings conducted by a subcommittee under Sen. Ernest Gruening of Alaska. Since then, interest in population has increased dramatically in the United States. It has taken two forms: making family planning services available to all sectors of the population—primarily, in the interest of public health, rather than for the purpose of reducing population growth—and an increased interest in the effects of population growth in the country.

The most significant event in focusing attention on the general question of population was the formation in 1970 of a Commission on Population Growth and the American Future, which was given the task by Congress of making a 2-year study of U.S. population problems. In March 1971, the Commission submitted an Interim Report which set the stage for its final conclusions. The report began with a fair statement of the problem:

"The time has come," it said, "to ask what level of population growth is good for the United States." It continued, "Our view, at this stage of our inquiry, is that population growth of the magnitude we have had since World War II has aggravated many of the nation's problems and made their solution more difficult."

If the conclusion that population growth in the United States should be reduced gains wide acceptance, there will remain the question: How can population growth be reduced within the framework of traditional American values?

To be answered, this question must be broken into two essential parts:

☐ How can prospective parents have only the number of children they want?

☐ If minimizing the number of *unwanted* children fails to stop population growth, what other remedies are open, and what are the advantages and disadvantages of each?

Reducing Unwanted Births

The measurement of how many children people *want* is a complicated subject, but one fact is clear: A great many children are born whose parents did not intend that they should be born. When this happens, it is often unfortunate for the children, for their parents and for society. Consequently, the first step in reducing population growth is to help parents prevent unwanted births through family planning.

"Family planning" is a concept which has replaced "birth control," a term used during the early years of this century when Margaret Sanger was put in jail for telling women how to keep from having babies they did not want.

For thousands of years man has sought reliable means of avoiding unwanted children by contraception—preventing the male sperm from fertilizing the female egg during sexual intercourse, or in other ways preventing a fetus from forming. Progress has not been as rapid in this field of medical science as in many others, partly because less effort has been devoted to improving the methods of birth control than to improving the methods of extending life by deferring death.

The principal methods of contraception include jellies and foams to kill the sperm; condoms and diaphragms to block the sperm; oral contraceptives or pills to make the woman temporarily infertile by chemical means; and the IUD (Intra-Uterine Device) to make the woman temporarily infertile by the insertion of a plastic or metal device into the uterus. None of these methods is completely satisfactory, although some are much more dependable than others. All have certain advantages and disadvantages, depending upon the individual, the cultural background and the circumstances.

In addition to these means of preventing unwanted births, there is the method advocated by some religious groups—the rhythm method. This method requires no pills, medicines or

Unwanted Births in the United States, 1960-65

One of the most effective ways of reducing population growth is to make it possible for parents to have only the number of children they want. That goal is far from being achieved in the United States. A study of fertility behavior in the mid-1960s indicated that almost 20 percent of births were unwanted. The proportion of births that were unwanted increased with family size, to the point that almost half of the children born to women who already had five children were unwanted.

Eliminating unwanted births, then, could have a dramatic effect on the birth rate. But population control advocates argue that even if unwanted births could be completely eliminated—a highly unlikely prospect—there would still remain the task of persuading parents to want fewer children. The baby boom of the late 1940s, the 1950s and the early 1960s was caused, not by unwanted children, but by an extremely high number of wanted children. Although today large families are not as popular as they were during the baby-boom years, these advocates argue that the baby-boom psychology could again become powerful unless further steps are taken to combat pronatalist influences.

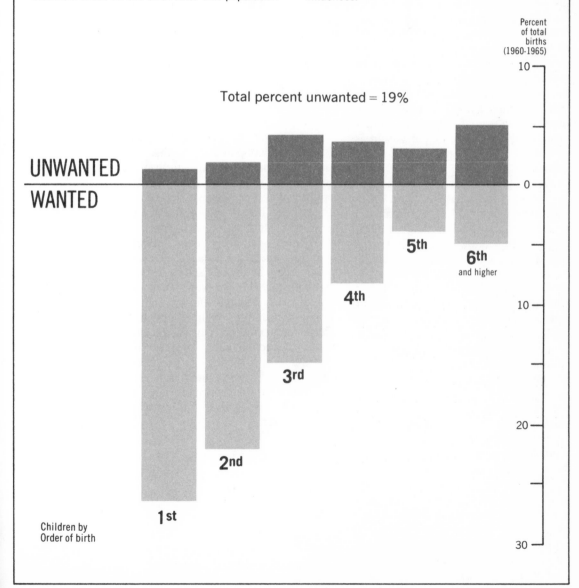

Percent of total births (1960-1965)

Total percent unwanted = 19%

UNWANTED

WANTED

5th

6th and higher

4th

3rd

2nd

1st

Children by Order of birth

devices, but relies on the identification of a "safe" period during each woman's menstrual cycle, and the avoidance of sexual intercourse during non-safe days. So far, this method has not been reliable because of the difficulty of identifying the safe period in individual women. However, recent research indicates that the rhythm method can be made much more reliable.

One of the major functions of family planning clinics, in addition to providing services and devices, is to help people determine which method of family planning is most appropriate for them, taking all factors into account.

It is a cardinal principle of the International Planned Parenthood Federation, the major private dispenser of contraceptive services, and a policy of governments which support planned parenthood clinics, that they must provide information and contraceptive materials on a confidential and voluntary basis. No forceful persuasion is to be applied to any person who seeks service.

Family planning is widely practiced in industrialized nations with high standards of living. Many have national health services which provide contraceptive information and services as a regular part of their community health programs. In the United States, family doctors have been the largest single source of information and service for family planning. In 1969, 1970 and 1971, as a result of a great expansion of federal activities and funds, hundreds of family planning clinics began receiving money from the U.S. government to support their programs. A 1967 law requires that by 1975 each state must provide family planning services to any person who needs them but cannot afford to obtain them through his or her private physician.

While government-sponsored family planning programs have been adopted primarily as a form of public health service, they have not been accepted without controversy. Some blacks are so opposed to family planning policies that they use the term "genocide" to describe their intended effect. The dictionary definition of genocide is "systematic destruction of a nationality or race." This is strong language.

Not all, or even a majority, of blacks go along with this charge, but researchers indicate that a significant number do, especially men under 30. Those who have studied the problem recommend a number of changes that could be made to ease the suspicions of minority groups that family planning is aimed at them. Among them would be the inclusion of family planning clinics in a general public health clinic program, to emphasize the health aspect of family planning instead of the population reduction side of it. Another would be the offering of family planning services to all segments of the population, not just to the poor.

Sterilization

For a growing but still small segment of the adult population of this and other nations, surgical sterilization seems more satisfactory than contraception. When a man or woman does not wish to bring more children into the world, sterilization is a sure and —for men—relatively easy method. The usual operation is called a "vasectomy" for the man and a "tubal ligation" for the woman. Both are virtually 100 percent effective in preventing conception. Neither operation affects the sexual activity of the individual. Although some progress has been made in reversing the operations when desired, particularly for men, sterilization is appropriate only for people who are sure they do not want more children.

The Genocide Issue—Two Views

by Dr. Charles V. Willie*

I must state categorically that many people in the black community are deeply suspicious of any family planning program initiated by whites. You probably have heard about but not taken seriously the call by some male-dominated black militant groups for females to eschew the use of contraceptives because they are pushed in the black community as "a method of exterminating black people." While black females often take a different view about contraceptives than their male militant companions, they, too, are concerned about the possibility of black genocide in America.

The genocidal charge is neither "absurd" nor "hollow" as some whites have contended. Neither is it limited to residents of the ghetto, whether they be low-income black militants or middle-aged black moderates. Indeed, my studies of black students at white colleges indicate that young educated blacks fear black genocide....

I designate the death of Martin Luther King, Jr. as the beginning of this serious concern among blacks about the possibility of genocide in America. There were lynchings, murders and manslaughters in the past. But the assassination of Dr. King was too much. In Dr. King, many blacks believed they had presented their best. He was scorned, spat upon and slain. If America could not accept Dr. King, then many felt that no black person in America was safe. For none other could match the magnificent qualities of this great man. Yet they were not enough; and so he was cut down by the bullet of a white assassin in a crime that remains mysterious, considering the help that the assassin received in escaping to a foreign land....

Let me explain why blacks believe any national program for family stability which focuses upon family planning is a desperation move on the part of whites to remain in control. Whites were not concerned about the family structure of blacks a century and a half ago. Then, blacks were nearly one-fifth (18.4 percent) of the total population. This, of course, was during the age of slavery, during the 1820s. Then, blacks were not free. They were no challenge to whites. Although they represented one out of every five persons in the United States, and although the family assumed even more functions for the growth, development and well-being of individuals then than it probably does today, American whites were not concerned about the fertility or stability of the black family.... Neither the size of the black population nor their circumstances of family life worried white Americans before black people were free.

But come the mid-1960s, when the throttle to the Freedom Movement was open and demonstrations for self-determination were going full blast, white Americans became concerned about the size and the stability of the black family. Daniel Patrick Moynihan tipped off blacks about what was in the minds of whites when he described the situation as "acute" because of the *"extraordinary rise in Negro population."* The size and stability of the black family was of no concern to white Americans when black people were enslaved. The size and stability of the black family is a cause for alarm among white Americans,

* Chairman, Department of Sociology, Syracuse University

Black Attitudes Toward Family Planning

Family planning in the United States, and especially family planning sponsored by the government, has stimulated opposition from minority groups. Some black leaders are even using the term "genocide" to describe family planning programs.

A recent study showed that this resistance is particularly strong among younger blacks, especially young men. In answer to the question, "Is encouraging blacks to use birth control comparable to trying to eliminate this group from society?", 28 percent of all those responding said yes, and among males 30 years and under, 47 percent said yes.

A major complaint about family planning programs is that they appear to be aimed at poor people, implying incorrectly that over-population is a result of excessive childbirth among the poor. Another point is that the major argument put forward by family planners for local clinics—that the practice of family planning will improve the health and welfare of those who take advantage of them—would be stronger if general public health clinic programs were more available.

On the other hand, the same study showed that family planning is commonly used by blacks—80 percent of all those responding to the survey said that they or their spouses had at some time attempted to control their family size.

Encouraging blacks to use birth control is comparable to trying to eliminate this group from society.

	AGREE	DISAGREE
TOTAL	28%	72%
FEMALES OVER 30	23%	77%
FEMALES 30 & UNDER	20%	80%
MALES OVER 30	27%	73%
MALES 30 & UNDER	47%	53%

requiring a national program of family control, now that black people are beginning to achieve freedom and equality.

Blacks, of course, would not claim that there has been an extraordinary rise in the Negro population. The black population in America has increased from 9.9 percent in 1920 to approximately 11.1 percent today—no cause for alarm. But then, maybe an increase of between one and two percentage points of the total population is an extraordinary rise if one believes it is.

by Dr. Louis Hellman*

Family planning services, financed by the government, have not been motivated by any desire to reduce the proportionate share of blacks or any other minority in the population, and the charge of genocide is a complete misunderstanding of what the program is all about. As a matter of fact, family planning has the potential of strengthening the absolute and relative power—economic, social and political—of minority groups if properly understood and used.

Voluntary family planning which enables parents to limit the number of children they have to the number they want and can support has been one of the keys to the improved status of people of all ethnic backgrounds. Nonwhites in the higher-income groups have small families—just about the same size as whites in the upper-income groups. It seems very clear that one reason they are in the upper-income group is that they did limit their family size. This enables them to spend more money on their own and their children's education, to live in better homes, to buy better clothes, and to do the things which most people with very large families simply cannot afford to do. Family planning can be, therefore, a means of getting out of poverty or low-income status to a higher-income status.

There is little doubt in my mind that any minority group which makes intelligent use of family planning—not to reduce their average family size below that of the majority group, but to elevate their economic status—can thereby become a much more influential minority group than it otherwise would be.

To deny any minority group the right of controlling their fertility while extending this right to the socially and economically privileged would be clearly discriminatory. Neither the majority nor the minority has the right to deny to any member of such minority the same basic rights to control fertility which are accorded to the members of the majority.

* Deputy Assistant Secretary for Health (Population Affairs), Department of Health, Education, and Welfare

Abortion

When a woman becomes pregnant but emphatically does not want to bear a child, she may seek an abortion—the removal of the partially developed fetus from her womb. Although opposed by some religious groups, abortions have been performed for thousands of years in a wide variety of cultures. The manner of performing them has varied from very crude methods—most of which are harmful or even fatal to the woman—to expert medical operations which carry very little danger if performed during the early weeks of pregnancy.

Abortion is legally sanctioned and used in most of the highly industrialized countries. Most nations of Northern and Eastern Europe have national health plans under which abortions are provided free, or at very low cost, to women who request them. The result has been extensive recourse to abortion in these countries. In Hungary, for example, the number of recorded abortions has been almost as high as the number of live births in recent years. In Japan, abortion was one of the most important means of bringing the birth rate down from 30 per 1,000 in 1949 to 18 per 1,000 in 1971.

Abortion has been the subject of great controversy in the United States. Some religious groups feel that the removal of the partially developed fetus destroys a potential human being and therefore contravenes higher law. Because of such objections, abortion has been legally restricted in most states to instances in which the health of the mother would be endangered by childbirth.

The existence of restrictive laws, however, has not stopped abortions; many are performed secretly and illegally, often by poorly qualified doctors or by completely untrained persons posing as doctors. The illness and death rate from illegal abortions is many times higher than from abortions performed by trained physicians. This fact alone has been one of the major arguments used to liberalize abortion laws in the United States.

It is estimated that approximately 400,000 legal abortions were carried out in the United States in 1971. The figures on total abortions have been particularly unreliable because of the illegality of the operation in many states.

In 1970, New York State repealed its restrictive abortion law and substituted a law which permits abortions in authorized hospitals and clinics on the request of a woman, provided the abortions are performed during the first 24 weeks of pregnancy. Several other states have liberalized their abortion laws within the last few years, and recent court decisions have nullified some of the restrictions which heretofore prevented women from obtaining abortions for reasons other than danger to their own physical health.

Population Growth and Family Size

The difference between a two-child family and a three-child family is tremendous over several generations. An average of three children per family will push U.S. population up to 400 million by the year 2014; the two-child family would mean 100 million less than that. In the next generation the difference would be even greater.

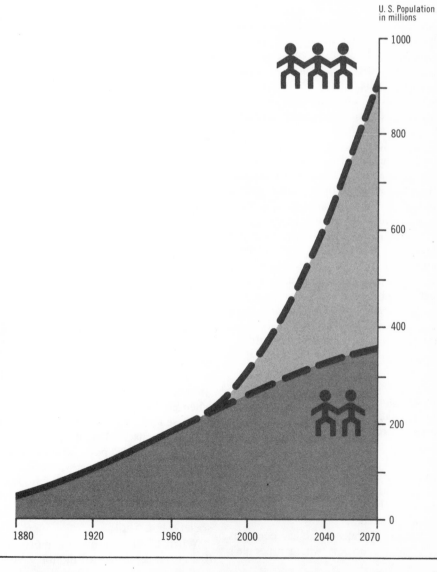

U. S. Population
in millions

Beyond Family Planning

Even though some family planning techniques are still controversial, the principle of deliberately limiting family size and thus avoiding unwanted births is almost universally approved. Sterilization has yet to win public favor, but its use is growing. Abortion is openly used in some cultures but opposed in others. If recent trends continue, potential parents will be able to use an increasingly wide range of methods to control their family size.

The key question, about which there is a growing amount of discussion, is whether the population problem would be solved if all these methods of birth limitation were universally available. The answer to this question hinges on how many children parents *want* to have. Obviously, if parents had a perfect way to have only those children they wanted, and if they actually wanted and produced three children on the average, the world or U.S. population would continue to grow rapidly. It would increase by about 50 percent each generation. This rate of increase could not long continue. And so the solution to the population dilemma requires still other approaches.

In a nation with strong democratic traditions, the idea of setting legal limits on family size runs contrary to what we think of as a cherished human freedom. It would face the strongest kind of opposition. Such limits have been proposed by some people, but no one has suggested how they could be enforced in the unlikely event that they were enacted.

Can effective steps be taken between the extremes of doing nothing about the population problem and seeking to apply coercive remedies? There *are* such steps. But the first question to be asked and answered is whether it is any of the government's business how many children people have. Is this not an exclusively private decision for parents to make?

What separates public concerns from private ones is whether people's actions significantly affect other people. If one family decides to spend its income on a fancy car and another on expensive clothes and rare steak dinners, these are private decisions. If one person wants to read radical literature and another conservative journals and newspapers, this too is a private matter. If a family has been brought up in a particular religion, it is free to continue that religion, adopt another, or follow no religion at all. If a person decides he doesn't like his region of the country, he has the right to move wherever he wants. These decisions and actions do not injure or unduly constrain other people or society as a whole.

But when a person in a congested city burns an enormous pile of trash, he creates a nuisance for his neighbors. When a factory dumps chemical wastes into a river that is the source of a metropolitan water supply or a recreational resource, it impairs the freedom of many other people. Obviously such actions cannot be sanctioned by law.

Parents have long thought of children as their private property, even though laws have been enacted to protect children from parental abuse. Similarly, most people consider the procreation of children to be a wholly private right, like deciding how many cars to buy.

But circumstances have changed. Burning trash and fouling the water were of no social consequence when people were spread far apart, but they destroy rights when people are jammed together. Procreation was a purely private affair in agrarian societies when there was plenty of good land and children might be economic assets. But when a society urbanizes and agrees to build schools and educate children at public expense, when it creates parks and playgrounds, pays for health and welfare costs of people whose income is insufficient and provides public services of all kinds, children represent social costs which must be borne by society as a whole.

When children grow up, moreover, the costs continue to mount. More money is needed for streets, highways, airports, police and fire protection, control of air and water pollution and hundreds of other social services. The private decisions of millions of parents thus exert a very large effect on society as a whole—both as to the nature of the society (how crowded it is, how rapidly it changes, etc.), and as to the level of taxes that must be levied to provide the necessary services.

There are other, nonmonetary costs that population dynamics impose on society. For example, a sharp increase in the population of certain areas, whether due to natural increase or due to migration, can destroy scenic beauty, jeopardize rare species of plants or animals, and threaten the balance of fragile environmental ecosystems. Here too, the procreative behavior of the individual has important consequences on the well-being of his society.

How can the public stake in family size decisions be expressed? Perhaps the most important voluntary means of achieving this goal is public education.

Population Education

Widespread education, particularly of young people—through the schools and television, radio, newspapers, magazines and discussion groups— may be the most important single means of influencing birth rates.

Generally speaking, people develop attitudes in childhood and retain them until and unless conflicting experiences intervene. One conviction they develop at an early age, without quite knowing why, is that they should marry and have children. They absorb this idea almost as an unspoken wish on the part of their parents, who often have a strong desire to become grandparents.

Not only is the expectation of marrying and having a family culturally transmitted, but even the *ideal size* of the family is so transmitted. This ideal goal influences (to what degree we do not know) the size of the real family people ultimately have, even though the "ideal" exceeds the number of children that they can afford.

When interviewed, most U.S. parents with less than three children say they have fewer children than their "ideal family size." Most families with four or more children say they do not want any more, but many have them anyway, often unintentionally.

The idea that large families are better than small families has been transmitted from parents to offspring for thousands of generations and is deeply rooted in our culture. Until recently, this tradition arose from the "imperative of survival." Mankind's immemorially high death rates meant that five or six or even more children had to be born to assure that two or three would survive to adulthood. Now, in our own century, this age-old imperative has been swept away—but the tradition of large families has not yet been uprooted. It has even survived the recognition that large families may now be contrary to the interest of parents, their children and society as a whole.

One reason for the continued drive toward parenthood is that children fill so many different social, psychological and economic roles. Research on the psychology of childbearing is just beginning, but one psychologist has detailed nine different values that may be satisfied by children. These range everywhere from economic utility, in which children are regarded as a kind of old age security, to novelty and fun, to helping parents achieve an adult status and allowing them to exert power and influence over their children.

Somehow, if people are to be persuaded to forego childbearing, substitutes for all these satisfactions will have to be found—no easy task.

For this reason, population education has suddenly become a matter of great importance to the human race.

How will the parents of this and succeeding generations unlearn the tenets that all previous generations accepted as true and necessary? Perhaps the process will not be as difficult as it seems.

If, after objective analysis, students become convinced that it is in their self-interest as future parents to have small families; if they become convinced that small families are also in the best interest of most children; and if they become convinced that it is in the interest of society itself for most families to be small, the ancient tradition may quickly give way to new patterns of family life.

Acceptance of Alternative Lifestyles

Lifestyles, in terms of marriage and family patterns, have varied greatly throughout human history. They have even varied substantially within this century in the United States.

The principal alternative lifestyles from which the majority of people make their choice are: (1) nonmarriage without children, (2) marriage without children, (3) marriage with a small family and (4) marriage with a large number of children. The proportion of people who choose not to marry, or to marry late, seems to fluctuate from one generation to another for reasons which are not entirely understood, and it differs substantially between countries.

Following World War II, the great baby boom, which was more pronounced in this country than elsewhere, seemed to reflect an attitude on the part of young people that marriage—preferably early marriage with many children—was the road to true happiness. This attitude had not existed to anything like the same extent during the 1920s and 1930s.

When the baby boom subsided in the 1960s, there was a slight reduction in the marriage rate and the number of children desired by married couples, but there was no return to the high percentage of nonmarried or late-married people which had prevailed three or four decades earlier.

Early marriage with three, four or more children is becoming notably less popular. It is now widely recognized that early marriages are the least stable and that the children of failed early marriages often must bear the consequences of their parents' mistakes.

Another possible change in lifestyle could be in the relationship between the family and other members of the society. The urbanization and mobility of American society since World War II has led to an emphasis on the "nuclear family"—father, mother and two or three children more or less isolated from the rest of the world, but often going in different directions and operating on different wavelengths. Experimentation with communes seems to reflect a thirst for large family units and a wider variety of peer group contacts than is available through the nuclear family. Other experiments may also prove fruitful, especially those which recapture the strengths of the "extended family" involving aunts, uncles, cousins and grandparents in a daily concern for each other's welfare. It seems certain that the search will go on for more personal lifestyles within a society that unfortunately tends to separate people from one another.

Changing the Roles of Women

The status of women in a post-industrial society is, without doubt, a key determinant of the birth rate. The more satisfying the work which women can find, the less likely they are to want large families. Women who lack the satisfactions which come from rewarding employment—a sense of belonging to a group, of self-esteem from being paid fairly for it and other psychic rewards—must find self-fulfillment in some other way. If, in addition to lacking employment, women lack membership in any social group with which they have rapport, they are strongly impelled to create a social group of their own by producing babies.

Enlarged and enriched job opportunities for women may be one of the most important factors in reducing average family size. Many women of childbearing age prefer employment at rewarding jobs to being fulltime homemakers. If our society genuinely desires to lower its birth rate, it must find more numerous, more satisfying and better paid opportunities for women, particularly those of childbearing age.

The movement toward equal employment opportunities for women in the United States is gaining strength each year.

It is bound to influence the U.S. birth rate.

Government Policies

Governments influence human behavior through tax and spending policies. They encourage businesses to locate in certain areas by undertaking the construction of dams, inland waterways, interstate highways and numerous other facilities. They influence business expenditures by permitting rapid tax write-offs for certain kinds of capital investments. And they channel individual behavior by levying taxes on liquor, cigarettes and jewelry.

Few governments have used their taxing and fiscal powers deliberately to influence population growth rates. But as the population dilemma becomes more acute, there is an increasing exploration of how these powers can be used to nudge people toward smaller families without limiting their freedom.

How heavily should a single person be taxed in comparison to a married person when both have the same income? In the past the federal income tax laws have placed much heavier burdens on single than on married persons. If income tax exemptions were limited to two children, would this harm children in families of three or more? If so, is there any way of achieving the intended purpose without hurting the children?

These are some of the questions which are puzzling many thoughtful Americans, especially legislators and advocates of a deliberate U.S. population policy.

The Impact of Crowding on Human Behavior

By PAUL R. EHRLICH and
JONATHAN L. FREEDMAN

How does crowding affect humans? Although much has been written about this question and almost everyone seems to have views on it, until recently there was little or no scientific evidence on which to base an answer. There was some research on rats—comparable to humans—and a poorly controlled

All things considered, crowding may not be so bad, but we should not assume it is of no importance.

crowded rooms in performing tasks.

We did discover that certain types of social behavior and personal feelings were affected. The striking finding was that men and women responded differently. In all male groups, the men became more competitive, more severe and liked each other less when crowded than when uncrowded; in all female groups, the women became less competitive, less severe and liked each other more when crowded. And in all effects disappear... whole and ... se produces ... separately. ... e effects, ... plex and ...

results and ... with great ... be consid-... disclaimer, ... t the effects ... ce that high ... r positive). ... t loss of effi-...

tween the density of people per of land and per unit of living A high concentration of people small area seems to have little tive effect; while lack of su space in the home is associate more crime, mental illness and ably other forms of breakdown.

•The effect of density is not — it probably depends on many factors in the situation. It is be crowded at a cocktail part friends, but unpleasant to be c in a doctor's office with strang

The main point at this early is for everyone to keep an open Accept neither the doomsday that crowding is inevitably ev the easy assurances that crow of no importance. For the re since the evidence does not s the former idea and actually su that crowding may not always bad, let us take a more op view of our urban problems. concentrate on solving the ec and logistic problems rather tha ing off the cities.

Shrinking Farmlands: Cities' Sprawl Stirs Fears of Acreage Shortage

Continued From Page One

ing through the center are fertile valleys of 00 square miles to the north and 100 square iles to the south.

"Beginning in 1950, the city and county en-uraged unlimited growth with the id was the key to progress alls Karl Belser, the from 1950 to 1967. lopments began pop the valley and the a boosting the valuatio to their potential co. farm value.

armers couldn't pay and still make a prof us encouraged furth ser continues. "In 1 ey became the home e than a million peo d been a beautiful, p sformed into an urban

500 acres, but the farmers contend a total 8,000 acres will be adversely and air pollution.

World Faces Job Crisi

JOBS, From Page D1

The job situation which the new workers are entering is alread flowing. David Morse, former general of the International L ganization, has estimated roug there may be as many as 7 people unemployed in the Thir which is just about the same of people as have jobs in th States.

Any traveler to the vaca the poor continents is b ser baggage car ist guid

trough in the business cycle, for which the governments of the day did not suitable remedies. But in the today economic

other factors; the tragedy of Viet has undermined American confid that we can prescribe for other ples, and made us wary of assu any responsibilities that could ome open-ended co

In 100 Years There'll Be 30 Billion of

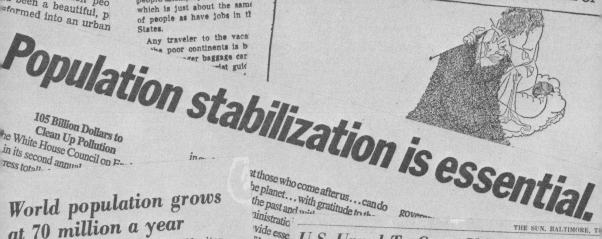

Population stabilization is essential.

105 Billion Dollars to Clean Up Pollution
he White House Council on F in its second annual ress total

t those who come after us... can do he planet... with gratitude to... the past and wid ministratio vide esse last year ing to F es and F

gover

THE SUN, BALTIMORE, T

World population grows at 70 million a year
Special to The Christian Science Monitor

Manila

h year, 70 million people are being orld's 3.5 billion population. holds three-fifths for the

U.S. Urged To Copy China Birth Polic

Family Planning Unit's Head Lauds Peking Control Program

By Muriel Dobbin
Washington Bureau of The Sun

Washington—An American population control advocate has urged that the United States fol-low the example of China in family planning.

He noted that Premier Chou En-lai of the People's Republic of China had set that goal seven years ago, and that family plan-ning in China—which has an estimated population of 800 mil-lion—was extensively supported

July, William H. Draper, Jr., whose group has helped raise $16 million for voluntary family planning, suggested that all na-tions should aim at reducing their rate of population growth to 1 per cent.

Free birth-control pills—in cluding a once-a-month pill said to be 100 per cent effective—de-layed marriage, and free and readily-available abortions per-formed without anesthesia ex-cept for the Chinese medical technique of acupuncture, or in-sertion of needles at strategic points, are part of the Chinese drive to reduce and stabilize its population.

Wrote To Chou
Mr. Draper reported that he had written to Premier Chou

suggesting that the chan communication opened via tennis might be widened in international exchange of mation on family planning

"Family planning and tennis are equally without ticular ideology or politic plications," declared Mr. I er, who predicted that i current 2 per cent world po tion growth continued. than 7 billion persons would in existence before the er this century—"most of the abject poverty."

The report of the Popula Crisis Committee was dev to reports on Chinese attit and methods regarding fa planning, these included an cle by Dr. Han Su-yin, the cian and author who linked cessful family planning to political and economic ema pation of women, and by E Snow, journalist and author reported on birth control p

THE NEW YORK TIMES

33 Top Scientists Ask Britain to Halve the Population

Continued From Page 1, Col. 7

mount of time left to us," he dded. "We cannot think of it a linear fashion—as if the next 000 years would be like the st 1,000.".

Runaway Demand Cited
he blueprint emphasized same old

will increase by a factor of 32 over the next 66 years.

"There can be no serious person today willing to increase the possibility, or indeed the desirability, of our accommo-dating the pressures arising from such growth. For this can be done only

move to encourage employment. A 100 per cent tax would be paid on those products designed to last for only one year and nothing on those lasting 100 years. Oth esrwo uldbe scaled in between.

normally a summaried td" according ho said that nothers were abortion uno-was endan-

The world population is now about 3.5 billion. The blue-print said that this number was probably the most th be fed for

by Hug Yu-press official in vernment, em-younger gener-chief target of oganda whic

Chapter Six

Three Models of the Future

Not only do we face the problem of securing adequate nutrition for the expanding world population; we also face the problem of trying to lift one-half to two-thirds of the world out of deep poverty.

Modern man is slowly becoming aware of his population predicament. He is gradually realizing that he lives in a most extraordinary and abnormal period of human development—a period of population growth so rapid that it cannot long be sustained. What, then, must he do?

Essentially, there are three principal routes by which man may come into more stable balance with his environment. The first would be the most tragic for man and many other species of animal life. It might be called "The Population Crash Curve."

Under this alternative, population would continue to double about three times a century until it overshoots the carrying capacity of the earth. Many delayed adverse effects upon the environment would then lead to a rapid population decline through extreme famine, excessive pollution, social chaos, high death rates from communicable and chronic disease, wars to hold or seize the ever scarcer resources of the earth, very low birth rates and other factors.

In the process of severely overtaxing his environment, man would also undoubtedly continue the process of driving numerous species of animals into extinction. These animals have contributed to an ecological balance which has sustained man through hundreds of millenia. Without them, we do not know what kind of an ecological balance would be possible for a very much smaller number of men in future centuries.

This Population Crash Curve is similar to that of various animal communities when some factor disturbs environmental relationships and causes the animal populations to expand at a rapid rate, overshooting the capacity of the environment to sustain the greatly enlarged numbers. Hares, deer, elephants and other mammals studied by ecologists have been found to follow this kind of a curve when predators are removed or, more rarely, when food supplies temporarily increase. The population of lemmings follows such a curve in recurrent cycles even when there is no conspicuous change in the environment.

No one can today predict with any assurance how likely the Population Crash Curve may be, or at what point the curve might turn sharply downward. The judgments of specialists in the field of resources, however, are that a crash would probably occur in the 21st century if population continued to double at its current rate of approximately three times a century. That is not off in the unimaginable future, but in the century during which children now being born will live most of their lives.

World population in the year 2000 would be not less than 6 billion; in 2033 it would be 12 billion; in 2066 it would be 24 billion; and in 2100 it would be 48 billion. It is highly unlikely that the earth could sustain 48 billion human beings at what we think of as a humane standard of living, and probably not at any standard of living at all.

If there is a significant chance that a precipitous decline—a new dark age of unprecedented bleakness—could come about if the human population continues to double at near its current rate, a substantial part of man's intelligence should be mobilized to avert it. "Letting nature take its course" cannot be depended upon to forestall the prospect that the 21st century may become the darkest century of man.

The Population Crash Curve

One way—a tragic one—in which growth could end is the population crash. If population continues to grow at the present 2-percent-a-year rate, sometime in the next century delayed effects of growth could lead to a sharp population decline through famine, pollution, wars and social chaos. Of course, the precise point at which the population curve would plunge downward cannot be predicted, but it is clear that the present growth rate cannot continue very far into the 21st century.

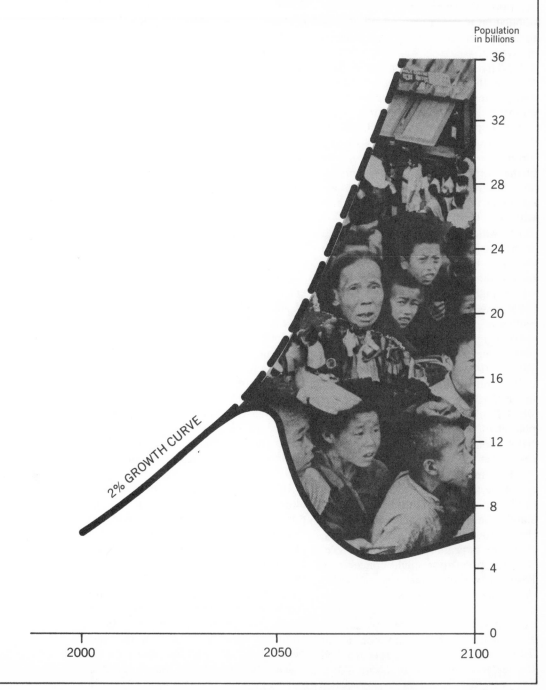

Population in billions

36

32

28

24

20

16

12

8

4

0

2% GROWTH CURVE

2000   2050   2100

A second route might be called the "Gradual Transition to Zero Population Growth." It is based on several assumptions:

☐ That we have not already passed the population level at which the earth can continuously sustain mankind at a reasonable level of health and culture;

☐ That man can and will slow down his rate of growth and level off his population within a limit which is continuously sustainable by the earth's ecosystem;

☐ That when world population does level off, there will be enough resources and political capability to achieve what an increasing number of scientists refer to with approval as a "steady state."

The lower and upper lines of this alternative illustrate well the nature of the world's population predicament. The lower line is based on the assumption that worldwide fertility rates will drop to the replacement level by 1985, which means that parents will be having just enough children, on the average, to replace themselves. It means that over most of the globe where high birth rates prevail, these birth rates would have to be cut by half or even more in a mere 15 years. And so great are the numbers of young people approaching their reproductive years (40-45 percent of the population is under the age of 15 in most of the underdeveloped world) that even when fertility comes down to the replacement level, there will be a second baby boom when the children of the first boom replace themselves.

The momentum of population growth is so great that even under this optimistic assumption, the "steady state" could not be achieved at less than about 7 billion people. This, therefore, appears to be the lowest level at which population might conceivably level off without markedly increased death rates or sub-replacement levels of fertility. The ultimate steady-state population of 7 billion would be reached under this assumption about 70 years after the fertility rate reached the replacement level, or about 2055.

The upper line of the Gradual ZPG Curve, 14 billion, is based on an arbitrarily chosen upper limit which would allow one more doubling of the population beyond the 7 billion level. Other assumptions could be used without greatly affecting the basic concept. This upper limit will be established by the limitations of the earth as a food provider, by the depletion of resources needed by industrial machines, by man's continued fouling of his own nest, and possibly by reaching the upper limit of man's capacity to manage his ever more intricate and interrelated economic, political and social systems.

Agricultural analysts are becoming increasingly skeptical that the world can adequately feed even 7 billion people. They point to growing agricultural stresses on the earth's ecosystem caused by man's continuing efforts to expand his food supply, especially through converting too much forest land to cropland, applying too many pesticides, and using too much chemical fertilizer. These excesses will increase erosion, eutrophication of lakes, extermination of animal species, dust bowls and other adverse effects on the environment.

Not only do we face the problem of securing adequate nutrition for the expanding world population; we also face the problem of trying to lift one-half to two-thirds of the world out of deep poverty. The industrialization of the underdeveloped nations would require, under present technology, very large amounts of natural resources and fossil fuels.

In 1970, a research project was aimed at determining whether a world population of 5 billion could find the resources to bring its average standard of living up to the 1970 U.S. level. Industrialized nations would continue to raise their standards but the non-industrialized nations would make up for some lost time and industrialize faster. Under these assumptions there could be some reduction in the gulf between the rich and the poor nations. The study concluded that supporting

The Gradual-Approach-to-ZPG Curve

A very popular concept today is the idea of zero population growth, or ZPG. As has been seen, however, the momentum of population growth makes immediate ZPG almost impossible. Even a gradual approach to zero population growth would be difficult. If worldwide fertility were reduced by 1985 to the point that parents were having just enough children to replace themselves, population would continue to increase until it reached some 7 billion people. If it took longer to reach replacement fertility, population growth might continue for another doubling, to 14 billion. There is considerable doubt that the world's agriculture, resources and environment could support a world population of 14 billion, or even 7 billion, so that this curve is highly optimistic.

Population in billions

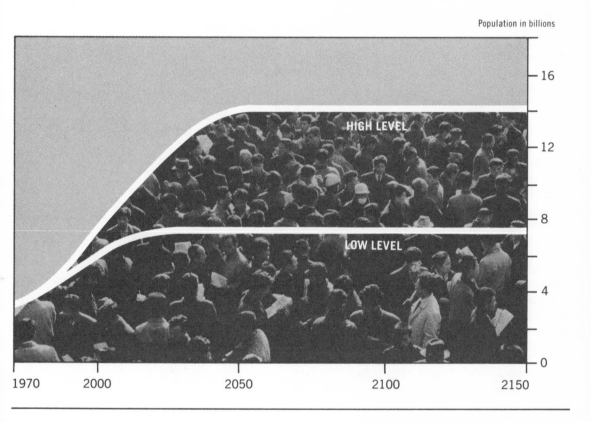

HIGH LEVEL

LOW LEVEL

1970   2000   2050   2100   2150

5 billion people at 1970 U.S. standards would require a worldwide level of consumption 10 times as great as the 1970 world level—a level well beyond the capacity of known resources and foreseeable technology.

If we cannot support 5 billion people at modern levels of living, it is clear that 7 billion, which the world will have under the quickest transition to a zero population growth rate, can only be accommodated under difficult and perhaps unacceptable conditions. The rich would continue to be very rich and the poor very envious. And if this condition were to exist at 7 billion, it obviously would be much worse at 14 billion—assuming that any such number of human beings could, in fact, be sustained by the earth's ecosystem.

The third possibility is labelled "The Modified Irish Curve." Its name derives from the experience of Ireland in the 1840s, when a disastrous potato famine occurred. Millions of people died, more emigrated and the remainder changed their basic way of life.

Judging by their actions, the latter group reached a harsh and unstated social consensus: They would not again overpopulate their island. Instead, they would reduce their dependence on a single crop, potatoes, by raising dairy cattle and livestock and developing other types of farming, and they would radically alter their mating behavior. The Irish thereupon shifted to patterns of nonmarriage, late marriage and smaller families, and they have continued this pattern to the present day.

The population of the Republic of Eire in 1970 was 3 million—less than half its 1840 population.

A similar fate might be in store for the whole world. Conceivably, the agrarian countries might overtax the carrying capacity of their land and, through a combination of drought, blight and other factors, generate famines which would repeat the nightmare of the Irish famine. Emigration, however, would not be a significant outlet, as it was for the Irish. The death rate might be higher. Food relief from the developed countries would be very small in relation to the need. The result might be a rapid shift in reproductive patterns. Such a shift might be preceded by, or perhaps succeeded by, a shift in reproductive behavior in the developed nations, which would bring about lower rates of fertility—possibly sub-replacement levels of fertility. Such levels might, thereafter, by common consensus become worldwide.

It is difficult to predict the point at which a hypothetically declining population would level off or whether the curve might turn back up. It might fluctuate for centuries. Some analysts have expressed concern that a long decline would be difficult to reverse. But a substantial downward readjustment in man's numbers—not too precipitous—might be the least hazardous alternative during the 21st century.

This alternate path might be modified to portray a smooth trend from the maximum height toward which we are now heading to some lower population which could maintain a high level of civilization in keeping with the earth's natural limits. This would require the application of a degree of human intelligence, foresight, mutual concern, cooperation and forbearance which has not been displayed by any previous human generation.

Anyone who believes these three models of the future are unduly gloomy is invited to try his own assumptions. He will find it difficult to employ any realistic assumptions that can make the prospects look much different from those set forth above.

The Modified Irish Curve

A series of disasters may cause a temporary decline in population, and shock the world into a consensus to keep population down. Such an experience took place in Ireland in the 1840s, when a disastrous potato famine occurred.

Before the famine, Ireland's population had reached more than 8 million, of whom 6.5 million lived in what is now the Republic of Eire and about 1.5 million in Ulster. In the 10 years during and after the potato famine, the population dropped 24 percent. More than a million people died from the direct and indirect effects of hunger, and 2 million migrated, mostly to the United States.

Largely through a change of marriage patterns, emphasizing nonmarriage, late marriage and smaller families, Ireland has kept its population down since then. In 1946, 80 percent of Irish men age 25-29 were unmarried. In 1969, 70 percent of the men aged 25-29 were unmarried. And the population of the Republic of Eire in 1970 was 3 million—less than half its 1840 population.

Population in billions

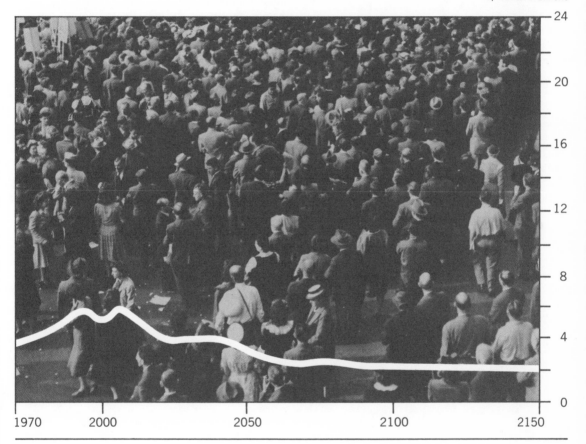

A word at the end.

Man's population predicament, to the extent that it is at least partially understood by people who have some concern for the future of mankind, seems to overwhelm them into inaction. They feel helpless before a crisis of such enormity. The situation is made even more difficult by the fact that most political leaders are preoccupied with finding short-range solutions to other critical problems. The population predicament is clearly not something that any national leader can do anything significant about in the short run.

Nevertheless, the enormity and the long-range nature of the problem should not lead to a fatalistic acceptance of whatever outcome may occur. The birth rate is controlled by the actions of millions of individual citizens, the vast majority of whom are under 30 years of age. It is the younger generation's problem.

The big question is whether the younger generation will find it in its self-interest and in the interest of its children to unlearn the reproductive habits of thousands of preceding generations and to substitute a pattern which can preserve the quality of life.

Appendix I:
Definitions and Computations

Every science has its own language and its own terminology. Throughout this book we have tried to define terms as they appeared, and often have avoided using a technical term where a more common word could serve. But precise definitions are important, especially when the subject is numbers. The information collected by demographers, and used to make judgments and predictions, is presented in a precise and careful way, so that it may be understood and used by anyone familiar with the definitions. But unless the definitions are clearly understood, data can be misleading.

There is another side to demographic statistics that, unless it is continually kept in mind, can also be misleading. That is the question of accuracy. Demographers are constantly aware that the numbers they use may not be very reliable, but sometimes laymen forget it. Even in advanced countries, where statistics have been collected for many years, the accuracy of numbers that represent the behavior of millions of people is open to question.

A good way to illustrate both the quality of demographic data and some of the major demographic measures is to describe how one of the simplest figures— the total national population—is determined. The basic measures used for estimating total population come from the **National Census.** Most countries today—there are some notable exceptions, including the world's most populous country, China—conduct population censuses on a fairly regular basis. Some censuses collect information on a broad range of subjects, while others are aimed simply at counting the number of people in the country at a given day.

If a genuine effort is made to count every person, rather than just estimating populations on a regional basis, the most common error in any national census is likely to be **Undercount**— the fact that some people just didn't get counted by the census takers.

The size of the undercount may be estimated by conducting a post-census survey, in which a representative sample of people are asked whether they were counted during the census. The proportion of those sampled who had not been counted gives an estimate of the size of the undercount. In the 1960 U.S. Census, for example, the undercount was estimated to be 3 per cent, or almost 6 million people.

A census gives a more or less accurate estimate of the number of people in a country at one point in time. But censuses are taken too seldom to be satisfactory for many uses. Often, estimates are needed of the population at times between censuses.

One way of arriving at such estimates is to use the **Intercensal Growth Rate.** This figure is computed by subtracting the population figure of the previous census from that of the current census. This yields the intercensal population growth. In the United States, for example, the 1970 Census population was 203 million, and the 1960 population was 179 million.

Intercensal Growth = Later (1970) Population — Earlier (1960) Population
= 203 million — 179 million = 24 million.

This figure is converted to an **Average Annual Growth Rate** by dividing it by the number of years between censuses (10 years in the case of the United States) and dividing that figure by the total population of the earlier census year:

$$\text{Average Annual} \atop \text{Intercensal Growth Rate} = \frac{\dfrac{\text{Intercensal Growth}}{\text{Years Between Censuses}}}{\text{Earlier (1960) Population}}$$

$$= \frac{\dfrac{24 \text{ million}}{10}}{179 \text{ million}} = 1.3 \text{ percent} \atop \text{per year}$$

The growth rate can be used to make a rough estimate of the population in the years between censuses. If the population had continued to grow at 1.3 percent per year through 1971, then the population for that year would be 1.3 percent greater than the 1970 figure, for a total of 207 million.

At this point it is advisable to talk about the use of rates for predicting where a population is going. Note that the previous sentence included the phrase "if the population had continued to grow at 1.3 percent." Most predictions or projections are based on assumptions of this sort: that some rate of change will remain the same as it was when last measured (or that it will vary in a certain way). It is important to remember that rates can change unpredictably, however. A given rate is accurate only for the time it is measured. Any extension beyond that period, especially for more than a short time, is open to error.

Another way to estimate population between censuses involves the use of three other measures:

The **Crude Birth Rate** measures the number of babies born in one year for each 1,000 persons in the population at the midpoint of that same year:

$$\textbf{Birth Rate} = \frac{\textbf{Number of Births Per Year}}{\textbf{Population}} \times 1{,}000$$

Similarly, the **Crude Death Rate** is the number of deaths in one year per 1,000 population:

$$\textbf{Death Rate} = \frac{\textbf{Number of Deaths Per Year}}{\textbf{Population}} \times 1{,}000$$

Net Migration is the difference between the number of people who enter the country in one year (immigration) and the number who leave (emigration):

$$\textbf{Net Migration} = \textbf{Immigration} - \textbf{Emigration}$$

Net migration can be either positive, with more immigrants than emigrants, or negative, with more people leaving than entering.

All three of these measures are complicated and difficult to obtain, especially for underdeveloped countries. They require that up-to-date birth and death records be kept on the local level, and that the results be forwarded to a central authority for integration on a national basis. Even in the United States, it was not until 1933 that all the states joined the federal system of birth and death registration, and many countries still do not have national systems.

Still, even partial registration can be used to estimate birth and death rates, and together these two indicators give a measure of the **Natural Increase** of a country (excluding migration):

$$\text{Rate of Natural Increase} = \frac{\text{Birth Rate} - \text{Death Rate}}{10}$$

Since birth and death rates are measured as so-many per 1,000 population, the difference is divided by 10 to yield rate of natural increase per 100 population, or percent.

In the United States in 1970, the birth rate was 18 per 1,000, and the death rate was 9 per 1,000. That means that the natural growth rate was $(18 - 9)/10 = .9$ percent.

Net migration can be converted to a "per-1,000" figure and added into the equation to yield the **Growth Rate:**

$$\text{Growth Rate} = \frac{(\text{Birth Rate} - \text{Death Rate}) + \dfrac{\text{Net Migration}}{\text{Population}} \times 1,000}{10}$$

In the United States in 1970, net migration was 400,000, or 2 per 1,000 population. So the total growth rate was:

$$\text{Growth Rate} = (18 - 9 + 2)/10 = 1.1 \text{ percent}$$

This figure can be compared with the average annual intercensal growth rate computed earlier. That figure was 1.3 percent; so the annual population growth rate in the United States has dropped compared with the average rate during the 1960s.

When it comes to predicting population growth over more than a year or two, demographers like to have even more detailed indicators than births and deaths. Most of these measures depend on a knowledge of the **Age Structure** of a population.

Age structure, as was seen in Chapter three, has significant effects on population growth. Basically, the rate of natural increase depends on two factors: the rate at which women in the reproductive age group are having babies, called **Fertility,** and the number of people that are actually in the childbearing period of their lives. (Natural increase also depends, of course, on the death rate, and some projections are based on assumptions that the death rate will change in a particular way. Others assume that the death rate will remain unchanged.)

In the United States, for instance, the children born during the high-fertility years of the 1950s, proportionately more numerous than those born in the previous decade, will be entering the ranks of parents during the 1970s and 1980s. Even if fertility remains at its present low level, the number of babies born per 1,000 total population—the birth rate—is likely to be quite high. Of course, if fertility drops below present levels, that would affect the birth rate also.

Fertility is measured in several different ways. Each has advantages and disadvantages, which make it more or less useful in projecting future population growth.

General Fertility measures the number of births each year per 1,000 women in the reproductive age group (15-44 years in the United States). This measure takes the age structure into account to a certain extent, unlike the birth rate.

The **Age-Specific Fertility Rate** eliminates the effect of age structure entirely;

it is the number of births per year to 1,000 women of a particular age. It can be computed (if the data are available) for each single year of age during the reproductive years, but it is usually computed for 5-year age groups: women 15-19 years old, 20-24 years, 25-29 years and so on.

The **Total Fertility Rate** is based on age-specific rates. It measures the total number of children 1,000 women would have if they passed through their reproductive years with the age-specific fertility rates of a particular year. For example, in 1968 the fertility rate for women 15-19 years of age in the United States was 66 births per 1,000; for 20-24-year-old women it was 167 per 1,000; for 25-29-year-old women it was 140 per 1,000. To compute the total fertility rate for 1968, a demographer would assume that 1,000 women would have 66 births each year between the times when they were 15 and 19, 167 births each year between the ages 20-24, 140 births each year between ages 25 and 29, and so on, corresponding to the fertility rates that existed for each age group *in that one year, 1968*.

Naturally, no group of 1,000 women is going to experience exactly the fertility pattern assumed in computing the total fertility rate. Age-specific fertility is likely to change over the 30 years a group of women will take to pass through their fertile period. So the total fertility rate is hypothetical. It is another of those measures that need the warning phrase: "if present rates continue."

There is a fertility measure that, unlike the total fertility rate, measures the actual number of children a group of 1,000 women have actually had. That is called the **Completed Fertility Rate.** It measures the total number of children born to women who reach the end of their reproductive cycle in the year of the measure. In the United States in 1968, the completed fertility rate for women aged 44 was 2.7 per 1,000 women.

At first glance it might seem that completed fertility would be a much more reliable indicator than the unreal figure represented by the total fertility rate. The difficulty is that most children are born to women in their 20s; so the completed fertility figure measures the childbearing behavior of women who had most of their children 20 years earlier. This makes it much less useful for estimating what fertility behavior is like at preent, or is going to be like in the future.

All of these measures of fertility can be incorporated into the process of projecting how population will grow in future years. But none of them is perfect, and assumptions about how fertility behavior will change in the future must remain no more than guesses. The U.S. Census Bureau publishes four sets of population projections, each based on a different assumption about future fertility behavior. Even then, frequent revisions have to be made as fertility changes. The Bureau has issued three sets of projections in the past six years: one in 1967, one in 1970 and another in 1971.

Appendix II:
World Population Data Sheet

Region or Country	Population Estimates Mid-1971 (millions) †	Annual Births per 1,000 Population ‡	Annual Deaths per 1,000 Population ‡	Annual Rate of Population Growth (percent) °	Number of Years to Double Population □	Annual Infant Mortality (Deaths under one year per 1,000 Live Births) ‡	Population under 15 Years (percent) ▲	Population Projections to 1985 (millions) †	Per Capita Gross National Product (US $) §
WORLD	3,706[1]	34	14	2.0	35	—	37	4,933	—
AFRICA	354[2]	47	20	2.7	26	—	44	530	—
NORTHERN AFRICA	89	47	16	3.1	23	—	45	140	—
Algeria	14.5	50	17	3.3	21	86	47	23.9	220
Libya	1.9	46	16	3.1	23	—	44	3.1	1,020
Morocco	16.3	50	15	3.3	21	149	46	26.2	190
Sudan	16.3	49	18	3.2	22	—	47	26.0	100
Tunisia	5.3	45	14	3.1	23	74	44	8.3	220
UAR	34.9	44	15	2.8	25	118	43	52.3	170
WESTERN AFRICA	104	49	23	2.6	27	—	44	155	—
Dahomey	2.8	51	26	2.6	27	110	46	4.1	80
Gambia	0.4	42	23	1.9	37	—	38	0.5	100
Ghana	9.3[4]	48	18	3.0	24	156	45	14.9	170
Guinea	4.0	47	25	2.3	31	216	44	5.7	90
Ivory Coast	4.4	46	23	2.4	29	138	43	6.4	260
Liberia	1.2	41	23	1.9	37	188	37	1.6	210
Mali	5.2	50	25	2.4	29	120	46	7.6	90
Mauritania	1.2	45	23	2.2	32	187	—	1.7	180
Niger	4.0	52	23	2.9	24	200	46	6.2	70
Nigeria	56.5	50	25	2.6	27	—	43	84.7	70
Senegal	4.0	46	22	2.4	29	—	42	5.8	170
Sierra Leone	2.7	45	22	2.3	31	136	—	3.9	150
Togo	1.9	51	24	2.6	27	127	48	2.8	100
Upper Volta	5.5	49	28	2.1	33	182	42	7.7	50
EASTERN AFRICA	100	47	21	2.6	27	—	44	149	—
Burundi	3.7	48	25	2.3	31	150	47	5.3	50
Ethiopia	25.6	46	25	2.1	33	—	—	35.7	70
Kenya	11.2	50	20	3.1	23	—	46	17.9	130
Malagasy Republic	7.1	46	22	2.7	26	102	46	10.8	100
Malawi	4.6	49	25	2.5	28	148	45	6.8	50
Mauritius	0.9	27	8	1.9	37	72	41	1.2	230
Mozambique*	7.9	43	23	2.1	33	—	—	11.1	200
Reunion*	0.5	37	9	3.1	23	—	—	0.7	610
Rwanda	3.7	52	23	2.9	24	137	—	5.7	70
Somalia	2.9	46	24	2.4	29	—	—	4.2	60
Southern Rhodesia	5.2	48	14	3.4	21	122	47	8.6	220
Tanzania (United Republic of)	13.6	47	22	2.6	27	162	42	20.3	80
Uganda	8.8[4]	43	18	2.6	27	160	41	13.1	110
Zambia	4.4	50	20	3.0	24	259	45	7.0	220
MIDDLE AFRICA	37	46	23	2.2	32	—	42	52	—
Angola*	5.8	50	30	2.1	33	—	42	8.1	190
Cameroon (West)	5.9	43	21	2.2	32	137	39	8.4	140
Central African Republic	1.6	48	26	2.2	32	190	42	2.2	120
Chad	3.8	48	23	2.4	29	160	46	5.5	60
Congo (Dem. Republic)	17.8	44	21	2.3	31	104	42	25.8	90
Congo (Republic of)	1.0	44	23	2.3	31	180	—	1.4	230
Equatorial Guinea	0.3	35	22	1.4	50	—	—	0.4	260
Gabon	0.5	35	26	0.9	78	229	36	0.6	310
SOUTHERN AFRICA	23	41	17	2.4	29	—	40	34	—
Botswana	0.6	44	23	2.2	32	—	43	0.9	100
Lesotho	1.1	40	23	1.8	39	181	43	1.4	80
South Africa	20.6	40	16	2.4	29	—	40	29.7	} 650
Namibia (Southwest Africa)*	0.6	44	25	2.0	35	—	40	0.9	
Swaziland	0.4	52	22	3.0	24	—	—	0.7	200

Region or Country	Population Estimates Mid-1971 (millions) †	Annual Births per 1,000 Population ‡	Annual Deaths per 1,000 Population ‡	Annual Rate of Population Growth (percent) °	Number of Years to Double Population □	Annual Infant Mortality (Deaths under one year per 1,000 Live Births) ‡	Population under 15 Years (percent) ▲	Population Projections to 1985 (millions) †	Per Capita Gross National Product (US $) §
ASIA	**2,104**[2]	**38**	**15**	**2.3**	**31**	**—**	**40**	**2,874**	**—**
SOUTHWEST ASIA	**79**	**44**	**15**	**2.9**	**24**	**—**	**43**	**121**	**—**
Cyprus	0.6	23	8	0.9	78	27	35	0.7	830
Iraq	10.0	49	15	3.4	21	—	45	16.7	260
Israel	3.0	26	7	2.4	29	23	33	4.0	1,360
Jordan	2.4	48	16	3.3	21	—	46	3.9	260
Kuwait	0.8	43	7	8.2	9	36	38	2.4	3,540
Lebanon	2.9	—	—	3.0	24	—	—	4.3	560
Muscat and Oman	0.7	42	11	3.1	23	—	—	1.1	250
Saudi Arabia	8.0	50	23	2.8	25	—	—	12.2	360
Southern Yemen	1.3	—	—	2.8	25	—	—	2.0	120
Syria	6.4	47	15	3.3	21	—	46	10.5	210
Turkey	36.5	43	16	2.7	26	155	44	52.8	310
Yemen (Arab Republic)	5.9	50	23	2.8	25	—	—	9.1	70
MIDDLE SOUTH ASIA	**783**	**44**	**16**	**2.7**	**26**	**—**	**43**	**1,137**	**—**
Afghanistan	17.4	50	26	2.5	28	—	—	25.0	80
Bhutan	0.9	—	—	2.2	32	—	—	1.2	60
Ceylon	12.9	32	8	2.4	29	48	41	17.7	180
India	569.5[4]	42	17	2.6	27	139	41	807.6	100
Iran	29.2	48	18	3.0	24	—	46	45.0	310
Nepal	11.5	45	23	2.2	32	—	40	15.8	80
Pakistan	141.6	50	18	3.3	21	142	45	224.2	100
SOUTHEAST ASIA	**295**	**43**	**15**	**2.8**	**25**	**—**	**44**	**434**	**—**
Burma	28.4	40	17	2.3	31	—	40	39.2	70
Cambodia	7.3	45	16	3.0	24	127	44	11.3	120
Indonesia	124.9	47	19	2.9	24	125	42	183.8	100
Laos	3.1	42	17	2.5	28	—	—	4.4	100
Malaysia	11.1	37	8	2.8	25	—	44	16.4	330
Philippines	39.4	46	12	3.4	21	72	47	64.0	180
Singapore	2.2	25	5	2.4	29	—	43	3.0	700
Thailand	37.4	42	10	3.3	21	—	43	57.7	150
Vietnam (Dem. Republic of)	21.6	—	—	2.1	33	—	—	28.2	90
Vietnam (Republic of)	18.3	—	—	2.1	33	—	—	23.9	130
EAST ASIA	**946**	**30**	**13**	**1.8**	**39**	**—**	**36**	**1,182**	**—**
China (Mainland)	772.9	33	15	1.8	39	—	—	964.6	90
China (Taiwan)	14.3	26	5	2.3	31	19	44	19.4	270
Hong Kong*	4.3	21	5	2.5	28	21	40	6.0	710
Japan	104.7	18	7	1.1	63	15	25	121.3	1,190
Korea (Dem. People's Rep. of)	14.3	39	11	2.8	25	—	—	20.7	250
Korea (Republic of)	32.9	36	11	2.5	28	—	42	45.9	180
Mongolia	1.3	42	10	3.1	23	—	44	2.0	430
Ryukyu Islands*	1.0	22	5	1.7	41	11	39	1.3	580

FOOTNOTES

† Estimates from United Nations. *"Total Population Estimates for World, Regions and Countries, Each Year, 1950-1985,"* Population Division Working Paper No. 34, October 1970.

‡ Latest available year. Except for Northern American rates, estimates are essentially those available as of January 1971 in UN *Population and Vital Statistics Report.* Series A, Vol. XXIII, No. 1, with adjustments as deemed necessary in view of deficiency of registration in some countries.

▶ Latest available year. Derived from UN *World Population Prospects, 1965-85, As Assessed in 1968,* Population Division Working Paper No. 30, December 1969 and UN *Demographic Yearbook, 1967.*

§ 1968 data supplied by the International Bank for Reconstruction and Development.

° Annual rate of population growth (composed of the rate of natural increase modified by the net rate of in- or out-migration) is derived from the latest available published estimates by the United Nations, except where substantiated changes have occurred in birth rates, death rates or migration streams.

□ Assuming no change in growth rate.

* Nonsovereign country.

[1] Total reflects UN adjustments for discrepancies in international migration data.

[2] Regional population totals take into account small areas not listed on the *Data Sheet.*

[3] US figures are based on Series D projections of the 1970 census and vital statistics data available as of April 1971.

[4] In these countries, the UN estimates show a variation of more than 3 percent from recent census figures. Because of uncertainty as to the completeness or accuracy of census data, the UN estimates are used.

NOTE: The completeness and accuracy of data in many developing countries are subject to deficiencies of varying degree. In some cases, the data shown are estimates prepared by the United Nations.

1971 World Population Data Sheet

Region or Country	Population Estimates Mid-1971 (millions) †	Annual Births per 1,000 Population ‡	Annual Deaths per 1,000 Population ‡	Annual Rate of Population Growth (percent) °	Number of Years to Double Population ☐	Annual Infant Mortality (Deaths under one year per 1,000 Live Births) ‡	Population under 15 Years (percent) ▶	Population Projections to 1985 (millions) †	Per Capita Gross National Product (US $) §
NORTHERN AMERICA	**229**[2]	**18**	**9**	**1.2**	**58**	**—**	**30**	**280**	**—**
Canada	21.8	17.6	7.3	1.7	41	20.8	33	27.3	2,460
United States [a]	207.1	18.2	9.3	1.1	63	19.8	30	241.7	3,980
LATIN AMERICA	**291**[2]	**38**	**9**	**2.9**	**24**	**—**	**42**	**435**	**—**
MIDDLE AMERICA	**70**	**43**	**9**	**3.4**	**21**	**—**	**46**	**112**	**—**
Costa Rica	1.9	45	8	3.8	19	60	48	3.2	450
El Salvador	3.6	47	13	3.4	21	63	45	5.9	280
Guatemala	5.3	42	13	2.9	24	94	46	7.9	320
Honduras	2.8	49	16	3.4	21	—	51	4.6	260
Mexico	52.5[4]	42	9	3.4	21	66	46	84.4	530
Nicaragua	2.1	46	16	3.0	24	—	48	3.3	370
Panama	1.5	41	8	3.3	21	41	43	2.5	580
CARIBBEAN	**26**	**34**	**10**	**2.2**	**32**	**—**	**40**	**36**	**—**
Barbados	0.3	21	8	0.8	88	42	38	0.3	440
Cuba	8.6	27	8	1.9	37	40	37	11.0	310
Dominican Republic	4.4[4]	48	15	3.4	21	64	47	7.3	290
Guadeloupe*	0.4	32	8	2.4	29	35	42	0.5	510
Haiti	5.4	44	20	2.5	28	—	42	7.9	70
Jamaica	2.0	33	8	2.1	33	39	41	2.6	460
Martinique*	0.4	30	8	1.9	37	34	42	0.5	610
Puerto Rico*	2.9	24	6	1.4	50	29	39	3.4	1,340
Trinidad & Tobago	1.1	30	7	1.8	39	37	43	1.3	870
TROPICAL SOUTH AMERICA	**155**	**39**	**9**	**3.0**	**24**	**—**	**43**	**236**	**—**
Bolivia	4.8	44	19	2.4	29	—	44	6.8	150
Brazil	95.7	38	10	2.8	25	170	43	142.6	250
Colombia	22.1	44	11	3.4	21	78	47	35.6	310
Ecuador	6.3	45	11	3.4	21	86	48	10.1	220
Guyana	0.8	37	8	2.9	24	40	46	1.1	340
Peru	14.0	43	11	3.1	23	62	45	21.6	380
Surinam*	0.4	41	7	3.2	22	30	46	0.6	430
Venezuela	11.1	41	8	3.4	21	46	46	17.4	950
TEMPERATE SOUTH AMERICA	**40**	**26**	**9**	**1.8**	**39**	**—**	**33**	**51**	**—**
Argentina	24.7	22	9	1.5	47	58	29	29.6	820
Chile	10.0[4]	34	11	2.3	31	92	40	13.6	480
Paraguay	2.5	45	11	3.4	21	52	45	4.1	230
Uruguay	2.9	21	9	1.2	58	50	28	3.4	520
EUROPE	**466**[2]	**18**	**10**	**0.8**	**88**	**—**	**25**	**515**	**—**
NORTHERN EUROPE	**81**	**16**	**11**	**0.6**	**117**	**—**	**24**	**90**	**—**
Denmark	5.0	14.6	9.8	0.5	140	14.8	24	5.5	2,070
Finland	4.7	14.5	9.8	0.4	175	13.9	27	5.0	1,720
Iceland	0.2	20.7	7.2	1.2	58	11.7	34	0.3	1,680
Ireland	3.0	21.5	11.5	0.7	100	20.6	31	3.5	980
Norway	3.9	17.6	9.9	0.9	78	13.7	25	4.5	2,000
Sweden	8.1	13.5	10.4	0.5	140	13.0	21	8.8	2,620
United Kingdom	56.3	16.6	11.9	0.5	140	18.6	23	61.8	1,790
WESTERN EUROPE	**150**	**16**	**11**	**0.6**	**117**	**—**	**24**	**163**	**—**
Austria	7.5	16.5	13.4	0.4	175	25.4	24	8.0	1,320
Belgium	9.7	14.6	12.4	0.4	175	21.8	24	10.4	1,810
France	51.5	16.7	11.3	0.7	100	16.4	25	57.6	2,130
Germany (Federal Republic of)	58.9	15.0	12.0	0.4	175	23.3	23	62.3	1,970
Luxembourg	0.4	13.5	12.6	1.0	70	16.7	22	0.4	2,170
Netherlands	13.1	19.2	8.4	1.1	63	13.2	28	15.3	1,620
Switzerland	6.4	16.5	9.3	1.1	63	15.4	23	7.4	2,490

Region or Country	Population Estimates Mid-1971 (millions) †	Annual Births per 1,000 Population ‡	Annual Deaths per 1,000 Population ‡	Annual Rate of Population Growth (percent) °	Number of Years to Double Population □	Annual Infant Mortality (Deaths under one year per 1,000 Live Births) ‡	Population under 15 Years (percent) ▲	Population Projections to 1985 (millions) †	Per Capita Gross National Product (US $) §
EASTERN EUROPE	**105**	**17**	**10**	**0.8**	**88**	**—**	**25**	**116**	**—**
Bulgaria	8.6	17.0	9.5	0.7	100	30.5	24	9.4	770
Czechoslovakia	14.8	15.5	11.2	0.5	140	22.9	25	16.2	1,240
Germany (Dem. Republic)	16.2	14.0	14.3	0.1	700	20.1	22	16.9	1,430
Hungary	10.3	15.0	11.3	0.4	175	35.7	23	11.0	980
Poland	33.3	16.3	8.1	0.9	78	34.3	30	38.2	880
Romania	20.6	23.3	10.1	1.3	54	54.9	26	23.3	780
SOUTHERN EUROPE	**130**	**19**	**9**	**0.9**	**78**	**—**	**27**	**146**	**—**
Albania	2.2	35.6	8.0	2.7	26	86.8	—	3.3	400
Greece	9.0	17.4	8.2	0.8	88	31.9	25	9.7	740
Italy	54.1	17.6	10.1	0.8	88	30.3	24	60.0	1,230
Malta	0.3	15.8	9.4	−0.8	—	24.3	32	0.3	640
Portugal	9.6	19.8	10.6	0.7	100	56.8	29	10.7	460
Spain	33.6	20.2	9.2	1.0	70	29.8	27	38.1	730
Yugoslavia	20.8	18.8	9.2	1.0	70	56.3	30	23.8	510
USSR	**245**	**17.0**	**8.1**	**1.0**	**70**	**25.7**	**28**	**286.9**	**1,110**
OCEANIA	**20[2]**	**25**	**10**	**2.0**	**35**	**—**	**32**	**27**	**—**
Australia	12.8	20.0	9.1	1.9	37	17.7	29	17.0	2,070
Fiji	0.5	29	5	2.7	26	22	45	0.8	330
New Zealand	2.9	22.5	8.7	1.7	41	16.9	33	3.8	2,000

WORLD AND REGIONAL POPULATION (millions)							
	WORLD	ASIA	EUROPE	USSR	AFRICA	NORTH AMERICA	LATIN AMERICA	OCEANIA
MID-1971	3706	2104	466	245	354	229	291	20
UN MEDIUM ESTIMATE, 2000	6494	3777	568	330	818	333	652	35

FOOTNOTES

† Estimates from United Nations. *"Total Population Estimates for World, Regions and Countries, Each Year, 1950-1985,"* Population Division Working Paper No. 34, October 1970.

‡ Latest available year. Except for Northern American rates, estimates are essentially those available as of January 1971 in UN *Population and Vital Statistics Report.* Series A, Vol. XXIII, No. 1, with adjustments as deemed necessary in view of deficiency of registration in some countries.

▲ Latest available year. Derived from UN *World Population Prospects, 1965-85, As Assessed in 1968,* Population Division Working Paper No. 30, December 1969 and UN *Demographic Yearbook, 1967.*

§ 1968 data supplied by the International Bank for Reconstruction and Development.

° Annual rate of population growth (composed of the rate of natural increase modified by the net rate of in- or out-migration) is derived from the latest available published estimates by the United Nations, except where substantiated changes have occurred in birth rates, death rates or migration streams.

□ Assuming no change in growth rate.

* Nonsovereign country.

[1] Total reflects UN adjustments for discrepancies in international migration data.

[2] Regional population totals take into account small areas not listed on the *Data Sheet.*

[3] US figures are based on Series D projections of the 1970 census and vital statistics data available as of April 1971.

[4] In these countries, the UN estimates show a variation of more than 3 percent from recent census figures. Because of uncertainty as to the completeness or accuracy of census data, the UN estimates are used.

NOTE: The completeness and accuracy of data in many developing countries are subject to deficiencies of varying degree. In some cases, the data shown are estimates prepared by the United Nations.

Photo Credits
Inside cover and Page 28: Black Star
Page 14: Harold Flecknoe
Page 34: Litton Industries